To the Reader:

It is a pleasure and a privilege for Black Ministry of The Lutheran Church—Missouri Synod, in partnership with Concordia Publishing House, to bring to you some classic books about the history of LCMS Black Ministry.

This year, we are thanking God for 140 years of black ministry in our church. These resources are intended to help you understand the history of black ministry in the LCMS and to help you grow in your appreciation for the work of our forefathers and foremothers on whose shoulders LCMS Black Ministry was launched. These resources tell the history of Sunday School classes, Christian school education, and Word-and-Sacrament congregations gathered around the historic confessions of the Lutheran Reformation: grace, faith, and Scripture in Christ—to the glory of God alone! It is the history of how the Gospel message changed the lives of untold thousands of black Americans only fourteen years from enslavement and thirty years from the founding of the LCMS. It is a history of great joy and immense struggles, as black Lutherans celebrated their heritage as Lutherans and stood up for their Lutheran equality and inclusion.

As this early mission work unfolded, the narrative was recorded in the verbiage and language of the time. These resources are the written history of those who lived in a segregated, prejudiced, and xenophobic society, especially in the Deep South, where most of LCMS Black Ministry started before spreading throughout the United States.

Neither I nor Concordia Publishing House endorse, embrace, or approve of such language. But we discussed the historic nature of the works and are reproducing these resources in the language of the writers. As the leader of LCMS Black Ministry, I asked Concordia Publishing House to make these books available again. My prayer is that you find in these books the historic narrative of a great number of Lutheran pastors, educators, and laypeople who left us the legacy of black Lutheranism, rich in its heritage.

We stand on the shoulders of those courageous, faithful men and women who have preserved our faith and heritage as Lutherans. They have left us a legacy that we must courageously fulfill for the future, for new generations of laypeople, educators, deaconesses, pastors, and other church workers for centuries to come—to witness of the glorious Gospel of our Savior, Jesus Christ, God's salvation for everyone who believes it.

As we look back 500 years to the start of the Reformation and at 140 years of LCMS Black Ministry, we can see we are at the threshold of a Reformation for these new generations to come. Like Drs. Rosa Young, Robert King, Richard Dickinson, Julius Jenkins, and others, we have a mission to accomplish. May God gift us with His Spirit to faithfully engage the world with His love, mercy, and grace in Christ.

Now, "may the God of hope fill you with all joy and peace in believing, so that by the power of the Holy Spirit you may abound in hope" (Romans 15:13).

Sincerely, serving Christ and His Church,

Rev. Dr. Roosevelt Gray Jr.
Director, Black Ministry
LCMS Office of National Mission

June 7, 2017

REV. N. J. BAKKE,
Field Secretary of Our Colored Mission.

ILLUSTRATED

HISTORICAL SKETCH

of

Our Colored Mission.

Sᴛ. Lᴏᴜɪs, Mᴏ.

CONCORDIA PUBLISHING HOUSE PRINT.

1914.

INTRODUCTION.

Kind Reader: — The Board for Colored Mission of the Evangelical Lutheran Synodical Conference herewith offers for your thoughtful perusal an illustrated booklet on the subject of "Our Colored Mission," expressing the heartfelt wish that it might be read by every member of the many congregations representing this vast body of Lutherans. This booklet is published with the purpose of acquainting you at some length with the work of evangelizing the colored race in our country, that is to say, of reporting the historical events of *your* mission work among these people, as it must be of vital concern to *you* as a Lutheran church-worker to know what progress has been made in this undertaking conducted by the Synodical Conference, of which you are a member. You have, no doubt, read, in our missionary periodicals, of the humble beginning and gradual unfolding of this laborious task among the descendants of Ham; you have undoubtedly sent up your sincere prayers for the success of this mission; you have surely also contributed your share for its maintenance at mission-festivals, as well as on other occasions. Now, then, this booklet wishes to picture to you, both by means of descriptive matter and by a wealth of illustrations, the exact origin, the steady growth, and the present-day flourishing condition of the blessed work you are helping to carry on among the colored people of our land.

This booklet was compiled and written by the Field Secretary of our Mission, the Rev. N. J. Bakke, who must be well known to you if you are a reader of the *Missionstaube* or the *Pioneer*. He is eminently fitted to write just such a booklet as this for the reason that he is *the veteran laborer* in this field. He began his labors in the interest of the colored race in the year 1880. During the past thirty-four years he has labored diligently and untiringly for the spiritual and moral uplift of the colored people; and the Lord has blessed his labors abundantly. You will observe, as you turn page after page of this booklet, how well informed he is in all the branches of this work; the reason is that he has not only grown with the Mission and heard and seen so much, but that he has been such an active participant in the work on well-nigh every section of the field. His statements therefore represent in a large measure his personal observations and his devoted participation in the performance of a task to which he has given by far the greater part of his life. You may rest assured that he has spared no pains to make this booklet not merely highly interesting, but also accurate in all its details. —

What is the purpose of this booklet? And why would we urge all Lutherans of the Synodical Conference to read it? The principal reason is, that we should like to have you become conversant with our Colored Mission, so that you will thank the Lord for what He has done for you and through you and your fellow-Christians for the colored race of this country. When you have finished reading the booklet, you will see that the Lord has richly blessed this Mission, that, in spite of many difficulties encountered at various times, it has been signally blessed by the Lord. Yes, it is He who has bestowed His blessings upon this undertaking; many immortal souls have been gained by it for Christ's kingdom. This blessing is noticeable to some extent even here on earth, but it will become fully apparent on the day of Judgment. Ought we not to attach great significance to the fact that the Lord has been so gracious unto us in permitting us to carry the glorious Gospel of the inestimable riches of Christ Jesus to the benighted colored people? Let us, then, give all glory unto Him and thank Him for His goodness and for the wondrous things which He accomplishes through us.

In connection with the purpose of acquainting you still better with our Colored Mission work, and thus getting you interested in it in a larger measure than ever before, this booklet would also impress upon you the necessity of continuing your efforts in its behalf, since there is still quite an extensive territory in which our best efforts and energies should be expended. You are to learn how much depends upon your individual participation in this work. You are to be invited and even urged to become more active and faithful in doing what you can toward furthering this cause of our Lord and Savior Jesus Christ. You know, of course, in what manner a Christian performs his duties toward the work of missions. The principal thing is *prayer*. A true Christian will pray for the success of this Mission; he asks the Lord to send more laborers into the harvest, to endow those already in the field with wisdom and strength to preach the saving Gospel message, and to grant His Holy Spirit wherever it is proclaimed, so that the poor colored people may accept it in true faith, and receive the end of their faith, even the salvation of their souls. The next duty devolving upon a true Christian is to support this Mission by liberal contributions, according as the Lord has blessed him. These contributions are necessary to give the missionaries their bodily sustenance and to build and maintain churches, schools, and theological seminaries, in short, to enable the Board to carry on the Colored Mission successfully, without check or hindrance. Surely, while perusing this booklet, you will reflect what great things the Lord has done for you, and this reflection will certainly stimulate you to help along this Mission in every possible manner.

May the good Lord bless you while you are reading this booklet with the riches of His abounding grace. Kindly note the contents of every chapter; and after you have read the book from cover to cover, make up your mind to read it once more. The Lord's blessing will attend you while doing so. Whatever surplus might accrue from the sale of this booklet will be used for the benefit of our Colored Mission.

By order of the Board for Colored Mission,

W. HALLERBERG.

CONTENTS.

THE NEGRO CHILD'S PRAYER.

I am a wretched negro child,
My face is dark of hue,
The bondman's curse on me is seen,
But — what's all that to you?

The haughty world on me looks down
With hate and sneer and scorn,
It kicks and curses, "jimcrows" me,
'Cause child of "niggers" born.

But thou, O white folks' Christian child
That lov'st the Savior dear,
Thou wilt not spurn the black child's cry
That rings into thine ear.

O lend me help, that Jesus' Word
In church and school may sound,
That grace sufficient may be mine
And to mine end abound.

Then blest shall be both you and I
Before our Savior's face,
When I shall thank Him with my song
For His all-saving grace.

O come, white folks that love the Lord,
Hear what the black child prays:
Bring Afric's sons to Christ, our God,
To live with Him always.

F. W. HERZBERGER.
Translation and last stanza by N. J. BAKKE.

A WORD OF APPEAL FOR THE COLORED MISSION
BY THE REV. H. C. SCHWAN, D. D.

The sainted Dr. H. C. Schwan, President of the Synod of Missouri, Ohio, and Other States, was from the beginning a warm friend and eloquent advocate of our Colored Mission. Whenever he attended the conventions of the Southern District of the Synod, he invariably paid a visit to the colored churches and schools in New Orleans, inquired into the conditions and wants of the Mission, and rejoiced at the progress which he found it was making from year to year. The writer remembers him in loving gratitude for the counsels and encouragements he gave him. At a time when the Mission Board was particularly financially embarrassed, which, sad to say, has often been the case, Dr. Schwan wrote in *Der Lutheraner*, among other things, the following appeal, which is still timely and applicable:

DR. H. C. SCHWAN.

"*If you heartily wish all men what God has already given you in His dear Son, then think, when you come to the words, 'Thy kingdom come,' in your next repetition of the Lord's Prayer, particularly and right heartily of the benighted negroes. Then see if there is not some coin in your pocketbook. Take it out and add it to that which other pious Christians give. Finally, take your pen and write to the Mission Board: Onward in God's name. Call laborers. Provide more room. Build a chapel. Here is a contribution. It shall not be the last, God willing. To Him the cause be committed. Amen.*"

THE EVANGELICAL LUTHERAN SYNODICAL CONFERENCE OF NORTH AMERICA.

The Evangelical Lutheran Synodical Conference of North America is a union of Evangelical Lutheran synods which adhere strictly to the Holy Scriptures and the confessions of the Ev. Lutheran Church, and hence are one in faith and doctrine. The object of this union is to keep the unity of the Spirit in the bond of peace, to exercise mutual watchfulness that purity of doctrine and practice may be maintained, and to conduct conjointly a mission among the heathen, particularly a mission among the colored people of this country.

In 1871, a committee met at Fort Wayne, Ind., to make the necessary preliminary arrangement for the first convention. On July 10, 1872, at the Ev. Luth. St. John's Church, Milwaukee, Wis., Rev. J. Bading, pastor, representatives of the following Synods assembled:

The Synod of Ohio and Other States.

The Synod of Missouri, Ohio, and Other States.

The Synod of Wisconsin.

The Norwegian Lutheran Synod.

The Synod of Illinois.

The Synod of Minnesota.

DR. C. F. W. WALTHER.   PROF. W. F. LEHMANN.   REV. J. BADING.
PRESIDENTS OF SYNODICAL CONFERENCE.

The Rev. Prof. C. F. W. Walther delivered the opening sermon on 1 Tim. 4, 16.

SYNODS BELONGING TO SYNODICAL CONFERENCE AT PRESENT.

In the year 1881, no convention was held. The following year it was resolved to meet biennially. On account of the controversy concerning the doctrine of the election of grace which was brought before the public at the beginning of the year 1880, the Synod of Ohio and Other States in 1882 withdrew from the Synodical Conference. Seven years later, not on account of doctrinal differences, the Norwegian Lutheran Synod also severed its connection with the Conference. It has continued, however, to send fraternal delegates to the conventions and, according to ability, to support the Colored Mission.

The Synodical Conference at present is composed of the following Synods, under the auspices of which the mission work

REV. C. GAUSEWITZ,
President.

REV. L. HOELTER,
Vice-President.

PROF. J. MEYER,
Secretary.

MR. H. A. CHRISTIANSEN,
Treasurer.

PRESENT OFFICERS OF SYNODICAL CONFERENCE.

among the colored people is being conducted: The Synod of Missouri, Ohio, and Other States, consisting of 22 District Synods; the General Synod of Wisconsin, Minnesota, and Michigan; the District Synod of Nebraska; the Slavonian Ev. Luth. Synod of Pennsylvania and Other States. Affiliated with this body are the following synods: The Norwegian Ev. Luth. Synod; the Synod of the Ev. Luth. Free Church of Saxony and Other States of Germany, and the Ev. Luth. Synod in Australia.

THE SYNODICAL CONFERENCE RESOLVES TO BEGIN MISSION AMONG THE COLORED PEOPLE.

The sixth convention of the Synodical Conference, 1877, was held in Emmanuel Church, Fort Wayne, Ind., Rev. W. S. Stubnatzy, pastor. For the Colored Mission this convention was of far-reaching significance. The gentleman who brought this subject directly before the convention was the Rev. H. A. Preus, for many years

EMMANUEL EV. LUTH. CHURCH, FORT WAYNE, IND.   REV. W. S. STUBNATZY.

President of the Norwegian Lutheran Synod and a pioneer among his people. He submitted the question whether the time had not come for the Synodical Conference to direct its attention to a mission among the heathen and, for the present at least, to take up active work among the negroes and Indians of this country. The question was turned over to a committee, which reported favorably. Under the invocation of God and with great enthusiasm the Conference unanimously resolved to begin and carry on a mission among the neglected and forsaken negroes of the land.

THE BOARD OF COMMISSIONERS FROM 1877 TO 1912.

The first Mission Board which the Synodical Conference elected, in the year 1877, consisted of the Rev. J. F. Buenger, pastor of Immanuel Church, chairman; Rev. C. F. W. Sapper, pastor of St. Trinity Church, secretary; and Mr. J. Umbach, treasurer, all of St. Louis, Mo. This Board had to contend

REV. J. F. BUENGER.

REV. C. F. W. SAPPER.

DR. F. PIEPER.

PROF. A. C. BURGDORF.

with the small and difficult beginning of the mission. It was a time of exploration and experimenting. The mission was on trial. Rev. Buenger died January 23, 1882, and the Board supplemented itself by electing the Rev. Prof. F. Pieper, D. D., Professor of Theology at St. Louis.

The second Board of Commissioners was elected at the convention in Chicago, 1882. It was composed of Rev. C. F. W.

Sapper, chairman; Rev. Prof. F. Pieper, secretary; and Prof. A. C. Burgdorf, president of Walther College, St. Louis, treasurer. Prof. Burgdorf served the mission in the capacity of treasurer till 1908, for 26 consecutive years, and shared its joys and sorrows. The Rev. C. J. Otto Hanser, pastor of Trinity Church, St. Louis, was added to the Board as the fourth member and as editor of *Die Missionstaube*. In various capacities he rendered the mission valuable services until his death in 1910. This Board was repeatedly reelected.

At the convention of Synodical Conference in Milwaukee, Wis., 1888, the Rev. H. Sieck, pastor of Zion Church, St. Louis, was added to the Mission Board as assistant editor of *Die Missionstaube*. But as he soon thereafter accepted a call to a pastorate in the Northwest, the Rev. Chas. F. Obermeyer, his successor in St. Louis, took his place as member of the Board. In the year 1897 the Board elected the Rev. Rich. Kretzschmar, pastor of Emmaus Church, assistant editor of *Die Missionstaube* and member of the Mission Board. From that time on the Board of Commissioners consisted of six members. At the convention in Cincinnati, O., 1898, Rev. Sapper resigned on account of ill health. For twenty-one years, also during the time that he was pastor in Bloomington, Ill., he had been an indefatigable worker for the mission as secretary, assistant editor, chairman, alternately with Rev. Hanser, and visitor of the mission field. He died in Los Angeles, Cal., July 23, 1911. In his place the convention elected the Rev. J. Bernthal, pastor of St. Trinity Church, St. Louis, and later president of the Western District of the Missouri Synod. In the year 1899, Dr. F. Pieper, having been elected to the presidency of the General Synod of Missouri, Ohio, and Other States, resigned from the Board, and Rev. Prof. L. Fuerbringer, Professor of Theology at Concordia Seminary, succeeded him. In 1898, the Synodical Conference elected a member from every synod and from every district of the Missouri Synod to represent the Board and the Mission. While these representatives are not required to attend the meetings of the Board in St. Louis, they are expected to look after the interest of the Mission and to advance its cause in the synod or district to which they belong.

During the years 1882—1898 the Colored Mission advanced into Virginia, Illinois, and North Carolina. In these seventeen years 16 congregations, which still exist, were gathered. It was a period of expansion under the administration of the mission-spirited reverend gentlemen Sapper and Hanser.

After the convention in 1898, the Board was composed of Rev. Chas. F. Obermeyer, President; Prof. L. Fuerbringer, Vice-President; Rev. J. J. Bernthal, Secretary; Prof. A. C. Burgdorf, Treasurer; Revs. Otto Hanser and Rich. Kretzschmar, Editors of the *Missionstaube*. In 1902, Rev. Hanser, on acccount of the infirmities of old age, ceased to be an active member of the Board, and the Board elected in his stead Rev. Aug. Burgdorf, pastor in Lincoln, Ill. A vacancy was caused again by his removal to Chicago, and the Rev. L. Buchheimer, pastor of the Church of Our Redeemer, became his successor. Upon his resignation Rev. W. C. Brink, pastor of St. Paul's Church, St. Louis, was elected. He died August 28, 1905. Rev. H. Meyer, his successor in office,

REV. C. F. OBERMEYER.

PROF. L. FUERBRINGER.

REV. J. J. BERNTHAL.

succeeded him as member of the Board. At the convention in New Ulm, Minn., 1908, the majority of the old members of the Board, because of other official duties, declined a reelection. — During the years 1898—1908 two higher educational institutions for the training of colored ministers and teachers had been established, professors called, and two college buildings erected. In the history of the Colored Mission this period may be designated as the Period of Higher Education.

The election of a new Board which took place at New Ulm in 1908 resulted as follows: Rev. H. Meyer, President; Rev. Prof. L. Fuerbringer, Vice-President; Rev. C. F. Drewes, Secretary; Mr. H. A. Schenkel, Treasurer; Rev. Prof. Geo. Mezger; Rev. H. B. Hemmeter. In the place of Rev. Hemmeter and Prof. Fuerbringer, who resigned, the Revs. Wm. Hallerberg and L. A. Wisler were chosen. Towards the end of 1909, Mr. Schenkel removed to California, and Mr. H. L. Doederlein was elected to the office of Treasurer. To fill the place of Rev. Meyer, who in October, 1911, accepted a call to St. Paul, Minn., Rev. Otto Laskowski was elected, and Rev. C. F. Drewes was chosen chairman.

In 1912, the Synodical Conference met at Saginaw, Mich., in the church of Rev. H. Speckhard, and the entire Board was reelected. The officers are: Rev. C. F. Drewes, President; Rev. Prof. Geo. Mezger, Vice-President; Rev. L. A. Wisler, Secretary; Mr. H. L. Doederlein, Treasurer (in January, 1914, Mr. Doeder-

REV. O. LASKOWSKI.   MR. JOHN H. SCHULZE.   REV. L. A. WISLER.
PROF. G. MEZGER.   REV. C. F. DREWES.   REV. W. HALLERBERG.   REV. N. J. BAKKE.
PRESENT MISSION BOARD.

lein removed to Chicago, and the Board elected Mr. John H. Schulze, 2211 Holly Ave., St. Louis, Mo., as his successor), and Rev. Wm. Hallerberg, Corresponding Secretary. During the years 1900—1912 colored ministers and teachers to a great extent replaced the white laborers, and the period may be designated as the Period of Transition.

"DIE MISSIONSTAUBE."

In 1878, the Synodical Conference convened in St. Paul's Church, Fort Wayne, Ind. At this convention the Conference resolved to publish a missionary monthly in the interest of the mission. The Rev. F. Lochner, pastor in Springfield, Ill., was

2

REV. F. LOCHNER.

REV. C. J. OTTO HANSER.

REV. R. KRETZSCHMAR.

REV. H. MEYER.

REV. C. F. DREWES.

EDITORS OF "MISSIONSTAUBE," PAST AND PRESENT.

elected editor-in-chief, and Rev. C. F. W. Sapper assistant. In January, 1879, the first number, under the name of *Missionstaube,* appeared in small octavo form, twelve pages. Two years later it had a circulation of 13,000. In 1881, it appeared in enlarged form with eight pages (quarto). Rev. Lochner withdrew from the editorship in 1884, and Rev. C. J. Otto Hanser succeeded him, with Rev. Sapper as assistant. Rev. Lochner departed this life February 24, 1902. During the year 1897, Rev. Sapper was chief editor, and Rev. Rich. Kretzschmar was elected assistant and member of the Board. But the following year Rev. Hanser was again at the head of the editorial staff. Since the year 1901, the *Missionstaube* has been published in the name of the Mission Board, and Rev. Kretzschmar was made editor, although Rev. Hanser was a contributor to the *Taube* even after sickness and old age had caused him to resign from the Board in 1902. He died January 10, 1910. He gave twenty years of active, self-sacrificing work to the Colored Mission. At the convention in New Ulm, Minn., in 1908, Rev. Kretzschmar declined a reelection, and the Board elected Rev. H. Meyer to the editorship, a position which he held till he removed to St. Paul, Minn., in October 1911, on account of his health. He was succeeded by Rev. C. F. Drewes, who is still editor of the *Taube.* (The price of subscription is 25 cents. The paper is to be ordered of Concordia Publishing House, St. Louis, Mo.)

"THE LUTHERAN PIONEER."

At the convention of the Synodical Conference in Fort Wayne in 1878, it was further resolved to publish a church-paper in the English language for the benefit of the colored people, and the Rev. Prof. R. A. Bischoff, professor at Concordia College, Fort Wayne, Ind., was elected to the editorship, a position which he held without interruption for thirty-three years. The *Pioneer* appeared for the first time in March, 1879. Though at that time the demand for English periodicals was comparatively small, the *Pioneer* found a friendly reception in many Lutheran homes and elsewhere, and the number of readers increased from year to year. Prof. Bischoff had the gift of presenting the Biblical Lutheran doctrines in a simple, clear, and convincing manner. He has, therefore, contributed much toward the advancement of the kingdom of God among the colored people of the South. When, in 1912, on account of sickness and infirmities, he requested the

Synodical Conference not to reelect him, the Conference voted him hearty thanks for long and faithful service rendered, and as a token of gratitude presented him with a check. The Rev. F. J. Lankenau, for many years missionary in New Orleans and first president of Luther College, was elected by the Board to succeed

PROF. R. A. BISCHOFF.
First Editor of *Lutheran Pioneer*.

him as editor of the *Pioneer*. (The *Pioneer* is published by Concordia Publishing House, St. Louis, Mo. Price, 25 cts. per copy.)

THE FIRST LUTHERAN NEGRO MISSIONARY.

The Board of Missions elected at the convention of Synodical Conference in 1877, issued a call to Rev. J. F. Doescher, traveling missionary in Iowa and South Dakota. He accepted the call, and was inducted into his office by Rev. F. J. Buenger, chairman of the Board, October 16, 1877, at the convention of the Western District of the Synod of Missouri held at Altenburg, Perry Co., Mo. He began his missionary activity at a missionary gathering in New Wells, Mo., which was also attended by a number of colored people. From there he journeyed via Memphis, Tenn., where he preached to the colored, to Little Rock, Ark., and remained there till January, 1878. His work in Little Rock was richly blessed. He succeeded in organizing a Sunday-school, which after his departure was conducted by the members of the German Lutheran Church. From Little Rock he traveled through the states of Tennessee, Georgia, Florida, Alabama, Mississippi, and Louisiana, preaching to the colored people wherever an opportunity was found, also on the large plantations. His first visit to New Orleans resulted in the organization of a Sunday-school in "Sailors' Home." He was ably assisted in his Sunday-school work by teachers and members of the German churches. But in March, 1879, he ac-

"SAILORS' HOME."

cepted the call extended to him by St. John's Congregation in the city under the condition that he be permitted to preach to the colored people till the arrival of his successor.

LITTLE ROCK, ARK.

To succeed Rev. Doescher at Little Rock the Mission Board called Candidate F. Berg, from the Seminary in St. Louis. He was ordained in Little Rock by Rev. C. F. Obermeyer, and entered upon his work soon after Easter, 1878. A chapel was erected and dedicated to the service of God August 18, 1878. St. Paul's Chapel was the first which the Synodical Conference built for the colored people. At the reopening of the school in the fall of 1879, Teacher E. W. J. Jeske, from the Teachers' Seminary at Addison, Ill., was placed in charge of the school. In October, 1881, Rev. Berg accepted a call to a German congregation in Indiana, and in February of the following year, 1882,

Teacher Jeske also resigned. The second missionary in Little Rock was the Rev. E. Meilaender who was installed on the 6th Sunday after Trinity, 1882. He died July 19, 1884. The Mission Board then called the ministerial candidate Geo. Allenbach, who was ordained and installed November 16, 1884, by Rev. C. F. Obermeyer. He served the mission in Little Rock six years, and the Lord prospered the work of his hands. In the summer of 1891, Mr. O.

REV. F. BERG. REV. G. ALLENBACH. ·TEACHER E. W. JESKE.
REV. A. POPPE. ST. PAUL'S CHAPEL, LITTLE ROCK. MRS. LEAH JONES,
Founder and Oldest Member

Kuhlmeyer, a student of theology at the Seminary in Springfield, was secured as supply. But this promising young worker died November 3 of the same year. Pastors Obermeyer and J. Miller, also Students F. Koenig, H. Frincke, Chas. Craemer, August Burgdorf, and Brauer, supplied the mission and assisted in the school work during the vacancies.

· The last missionary in Little Rock was Rev. C. Ruesskamp. He was ordained to the ministry August 21, 1892, by his former pastor, Rev. H. H. Walker, York, Pa., and was inducted into office at Little Rock by Rev. J. Miller, September 25. About three years later, October, 1895, he resigned, and the Mission Board, being just as discouraged as the missionary, resolved to abandon the field and to sell the property. Some of the members, however, adhered to the Lutheran Church. They gathered together in the home of one of the members, read the Bible, recited the Catechism, and sang Lutheran hymns. Now and then the pastor of the

REV. L. WAHL.

German Lutheran Church preached to them and administered the Lord's Supper. Upon invitation of the white Lutheran church the colored Lutherans attended the English services there for a time. For many years now the Rev. Ad. Poppe has administered the means of grace to this little flock in a private house. They are still hoping to have a missionary of their own again in their midst, and, God willing, their hopes shall not be put to shame.

MOBILE, ALA.

From New Orleans Rev. Doescher made several journeys to adjacent states. In Mobile, Ala., he organized a colored Lutheran Sunday-school, which was continued by the members of the white Lutheran church till the arrival of the missionary, Rev. Leopold

C. A. Wahl. Rev. Wahl had been for eleven years in the service of the Hermannsburg Missionary Society in India, but on account of doctrinal differences resigned and came to the United States. After a theological examination before the sainted Dr. Walther he accepted a call to the Colored Mission, and was sent by the Board to Mobile. He began his work in that city in March, 1880, in a store-room. The labor was not in vain. The school he opened was well attended, and a few adults, besides children, came to the services. He also prepared a small class for confirmation. But after a year and a half he accepted a call to the German Lutheran church in that city. Having neither means nor men, the Board was unable to continue the mission in Mobile. For the same reason the work has not been resumed.

NEW ORLEANS, LA.

1. Mount Zion.

In 1880, the writer, a graduate of the Seminary in St. Louis, was called to the Negro Mission, to succeed Rev. Doescher in New Orleans. On the 7th of November he was ordained by Rev. J. F. Buenger in Immanuel Church, St. Louis, and a week later installed in "Sailors' Home" by Rev. Doescher. "Sailors' Home" was an old dilapidated brick structure, three stories high, and contained about 75 large and small rooms. A large hall in this building had been primitively arranged for the Colored Mission. A picture of it as it appeared at that time cannot be obtained. Rev. Doescher had confirmed one man and a few poor women, some of them sickly. He named the congregation "Mount Zion." A colored man by the name of Rev. Polk, of Baltimore, conducted the school for a few months. He was succeeded by Miss Louise Watson, a colored lady, who was a Lutheran by profession, but a Catholic at heart. In September, 1881, Mr. Eugene R. Vix, a graduate of Addison, Ill., was placed in charge of the school, with Miss Watson as assistant. Teacher Vix has presided over that same school with conscientious fidelity for over thirty-two years. On account of the controversy concerning the doctrine of election, Rev. Doescher, in 1882, severed his connection with the Synodical Conference and joined the Ohio Synod, and the members he had confirmed followed him. Some, however, returned. The new missionary labored for two years with small success in "Sailors' Home." Only two women were gained, one of whom is still a member of Mount Zion. Towards the end of the year 1882, the Board purchased a large old church at the corner of Thalia and Franklin, repaired it, and arranged it for church and school. On December 3, it was dedicated. From that time on the work of the Lord began to prosper.

The writer served Mount Zion in connection with St. Paul's Station until August, 1891. He was succeeded by Rev. F. J. Lankenau, from the Seminary in Springfield, who was ordained in Mount Zion on the 13th Sunday after Trinity that year. His

OLD MOUNT ZION CHURCH.

successor in Mount Zion, Rev. E. W. Kuss, who was transferred from the abandoned Carrollton field, was installed May 1, 1894. Teacher D. Meibohm, who began his work in the school by the side of Mr. Vix, in November, 1893, can look back upon more than twenty years of faithful service in Mount Zion. The Board bought a valuable building site adjoining the old property, and in 1895 erected a commodious school building, which was dedicated May 12. A year later the old church was torn down and a new edifice erected under the direction of Rev. Kuss. Of all the church buildings in our Mission Mount Zion is the largest and handsomest. The congregation contributed nearly one half of the expenses. It was set apart for the service of God February 21, 1897. In the spring of the same year Rev. Kuss accepted a call to the German Zion Church of the city, and during the vacancy Rev. Lankenau served the congregation. Mr. N. P. Burkhalter, who had attended the Seminary in Springfield for a time, was in charge of the primary classes of the school from 1889 to October, 1890, and Emmanuel Burthlong from 1890 to 1891, both colored. Emmanuel was a gifted, pious youth who had been educated in St. Paul's School. In the fall of 1891 he was admitted to the Seminary in Springfield to prepare himself for the ministry. He was our first colored Lutheran student from a colored Lutheran

PRESENT MOUNT ZION CHURCH AND SCHOOL.

congregation. For a year he served as vicar in North Carolina. A few months before the completion of his theological studies he took sick and was brought home, where he died February 28, 1897.

In the year 1900, the Mission Board called the ministerial candidate from the Seminary in St. Louis, Carl Kretzschmar, to Mount Zion. He was ordained in Mount Zion September 2. Owing to the illness of his wife he resigned in the spring of 1907 and accepted a call to Hastings, Nebr. He was succeeded in 1908 by Rev. Ed. Krause, a graduate of Concordia Seminary, St. Louis, who was ordained to the office of the holy ministry on the 12th Sunday after Trinity. On account of his health he accepted a call to Nebraska in August, 1910, and the congregation was again without a pastor. During the long vacancy that ensued, Rev. G. M. Kramer acted as supply. These vacancies were detrimental to the growth of the church. The members became disheartened and neglectful, and amalgamation with the Bethlehem Church was seriously considered. For six months, 1911—1912, the writer assisted Rev. Kramer in his work in Mount Zion. During that

TEACHER E. R. VIX.

TEACHER D. MEIBOHM.

TEACHER A. BERGER.

REV. E. W. KUSS.

REV. K. KRETZSCHMAR.

REV. E. KRAUSE.

REV. A. O. FRIEDRICH.

time the congregation, for the first time in the history of the Mission, elected and called its own pastor under the direction of the Mission Board. The Rev. Alb. O. Friedrich accepted the call and was installed July 12, 1912. Under his pastoral care the congregation is making satisfactory progress. In the summer of 1913 the schoolhouse was enlarged and a third teacher added, Mr. A. Berger, a graduate of Luther College, New Orleans, and Immanuel College, Greensboro, who was installed August 29, 1913.

2. St. Paul's.

An attempt was made by Rev. Doescher to establish another station among the Creoles. Upon rented grounds, on Claiborne Street, a small chapel of rough planks was built with

OLD ST. PAUL'S CHAPEL AND SCHOOL.

the surplus money of the yellow fever fund. A Sunday-school was organized and conducted by Teacher Chas. Sauer of the German St. Paul's Church. But the attendance was so discouraging that the Mission Board decided to discontinue the work and to sell the chapel. Upon the arrival of the writer at New Orleans the missionary work was resumed, the Board consenting to give it another trial. He served the station till his removal to North Carolina in 1891. In January, 1881, Teacher Charles Berg, who for a few months had assisted in the school at Little Rock, was transferred to New Orleans and placed in charge of the Claiborne school. Only 7 children attended the opening of the school, but in a short time he had an enrollment of about 70. Mr. Berg was an excellent teacher and a capable coworker, and his labor was signally blest. The first members and founders of St. Paul's Congregation were children educated in his school. After seven years the Lord summoned His faithful servant to His heavenly

ST. PAUL'S PRESENT CHURCH EDIFICE.

mansions. He died March 9, 1888, and was buried in the cemetery of the Ev. Luth. St. John's Church. In 1883, the Board bought a lot on Annette Street, near Claiborne, and the chapel was moved there and repaired. The enemies, and they were many, called the chapel "The Chicken Coop," but the friends, St. Paul's Chapel.

Appeals were repeatedly made for more room to accommodate the growing school and congregation. At last the Mission Board yielded, though its hands were tied by a resolution of the Synodical Conference. The work on the new church building was in progress when that body met at Milwaukee, Wis., in 1888. The convention promptly approved the action of the Board. The church was dedicated September 23 of the same year. On the 14th Sunday after Trinity the Rev. F. J. Lankenau, the successor of the writer, delivered his introductory sermon in St. Paul's. While a student in Springfield, he had supplied the mission in Meherrin, Va., for a year and St. Paul's School after the death of Mr. Berg. For about two years Rev. F. W. Siebelitz, ordained in St. John's Church, New Orleans, November 14, 1897, was his assistant in church and school. After seventeen years of active, consecrated service in the Mission in the capacity of missionary, teacher, and president of Luther College, Rev. Lankenau accepted a call to Napoleon, O., and delivered his valedictory sermon in St. Paul's on the 12th Sunday after Trinity, 1908. During the vacancy

REV. F. J. LANKENAU.   REV. ED. H. SCHMIDT.

the congregation was supplied by Prof. F. Wenger, his successor as president of Luther College. In the year 1909, the Mission Board called the Rev. Alb. Witt, of Lockport, N. Y., who was inducted into his office on the 26th of September. Having served the congregation for about nine months, he accepted the call extended to him by St. John's Church in New Orleans. The present pastor and missionary is the Rev. Ed. H. Schmidt, formerly in Napoleonville, La. He entered upon his work at St. Paul's October 23, 1910. Despite the vacancies and changes occurring from 1908 to 1910, which proved quite detrimental, St. Paul's is our largest congregation, having at the end of 1913 a membership of 380 baptized members and 158 communicant members.

At the convention of the Synodical Conference in St. Paul, Minn., 1890, it was resolved to build two schoolhouses for our Mission in New Orleans, for St. Paul's and Bethlehem. The resolution was carried out without delay. St. Paul's School was dedicated March 8, 1891. After the death of Teacher Berg the theological student F. J. Lankenau taught school there till the end of the school-year. Then the Board called the Addison graduate A. Scheffler, who entered upon his work in September, 1888. During the Christmas vacation 1890, the teacher mysteriously vanished. Teacher J. Kaufmann succeeded him in January, 1891, and taught until a few days before his death, May 10th of the same year. He was buried by the side of his

TEACHER CHAS. BERG. TEACHER C. LEMKE. TEACHER E. H. HEINTZEN.

TEACHER AARON WILEY. TEACHER W. SEEBERRY.

friend, C. Berg, in St. John's Cemetery. On the 14th Sunday after Trinity, 1891, Teacher C. Lemke, also a graduate of Addison Seminary, succeeded him, but after about three years he resigned to accept a call to Buffalo, N. Y. During the vacancy, Rev. Lankenau himself taught the school with the assistance of a lady teacher. In December, 1896, the Board transferred Teacher C. Niewedde from Bethlehem Station to St. Paul's, and the following year Rev. Siebelitz was called as assistant pastor and teacher of the primary department. Both resigned in 1899. The Addison graduate H. Heintzen was installed September 2, 1900, and taught the school for four years. Teacher R. A. Wilde, of the Addison

Seminary, was placed in charge of the school on the 15th of September, 1902, and Teacher L. Fuhrmann on the 3d of January, 1904. The latter died in Chicago September 26th of that year. Since then graduates of Luther College, New Orleans, have conducted the school: Mr. Napoleon Seeberry, from the 17th Sunday after Trinity, 1904; Mr. Aaron Wiley, Jr., from September 2, 1906; Mr. W. Seeberry from September, 1908. The last two, together with John Thompson, who was installed September 21, 1913, and Miss Sylvina Raymond, are the present teachers. From time to time the Misses Trog, Holland, Lankenau, Hamann, Edna Walters, Edna Thomas, and Sophie Raymond, the last three graduates of Luther College, have been assistants.

REV. AUG. BURGDORF.

TRINITY CHURCH.

3. Trinity.

In the year 1884, the Synodical Conference resolved to send another missionary to New Orleans, and the Mission Board called the St. Louis graduate Aug. Burgdorf. On the 18th Sunday after Trinity, October 4, 1885, he was ordained in Mount Zion Church, New Orleans, by Rev. T. Stiemke, President of the Southern District. He began his work in Carrollton, a suburb of New Orleans. The Board bought an old church belonging to the German Evangelical Congregation, with bell and other equipments, for $600. The steeple, being ornamented with a rooster, the church was generally known as the "Rooster Church." It was dedicated February 21, 1886. Rev. Burgdorf opened a school, which in a short time had enrolled 90 children. In September of the same year the Addison graduate W. Joeckel took charge of the school and remained until the end of the school-year 1889. His successor was Louis E. Gilster, from the Seminary in Addison, who resigned at close of school in 1890. He, in turn, was succeeded by Mr. J. Moser, a member of the English Lutheran congregation at Gravelton, Mo., who had studied for a time at the Seminary in Springfield. After a year's work he also resigned. In 1893, the Board called a graduate from the Seminary in St. Louis, E. W. Kuss. He was ordained by Rev. Burgdorf September 10. The visible fruits of the work in Carrollton were small, and the Mission Board, upon the advice of the missionaries, decided to abandon the field, and in 1894 the Board transferred Rev. Kuss to Mount Zion, New Orleans.

4. Bethlehem.

Having been relieved of the school work at Carrollton, Rev. Burgdorf began to devote much of his time to the establishment of a mission in the fourth district of the city. At the house of a family which had been attending Mount Zion Church he gave catechetical instruction to a few adults. On the corner of Washington and Dryades, adjoining "Noah's Ark," an old dilapidated two-story frame building of unsavory repute, the Board bought a building site, and a chapel, arranged for church and school, was erected. It was dedicated on the second Sunday after Epiphany, 1888, and is known in the history of our Mission as Bethlehem Chapel. The school, conducted by the missionary, was soon filled with children. On the 15th Sunday after Trinity, 1888, the Addison graduate E. W. Rischow was installed into his office and labored in the school till November 15, 1903. On account of his health Rev. Burgdorf, in 1895, after a decade of untiring, self-sacrificing labor, severed his connection with the Mission in New Orleans. A year of recuperation in the mountains of Tennessee partly restored his health, and he took up work among the colored people of Atlanta, Ga., which sickness, however, compelled him to give up. Having devoted another year, partly to missionary work in Wilmington, N. C., partly to a lengthy visit to the churches and schools of our Mission in that state, he accepted a call to Lincoln, Ill. To succeed him, the Mission Board called Rev. J. W. F. Kossmann, who as a student in Springfield had been active in the Mission. He entered upon his work at Bethlehem November 10, 1895, and served successfully till September, 1906, eleven years, when he accepted a call to Convoy, O. The present pastor of the congregation is Rev. G. M. Kramer, a St. Louis graduate, who entered the Mission on the 12th Sunday after Trinity, 1907.

3

REV. J. W. F. KOSSMANN.   REV. G. M. KRAMER.   TEACHER E. W. RISCHOW.
TEACHER NAP. SEEBERRY.   BETHLEHEM CHAPEL.   TEACHER W. SCHRIEBER.
TEACHER L. POLLERT.   TEACHER C. F. LANGE.

Pursuant to a resolution of the Synodical Conference in 1890, a two-story commodious schoolhouse was erected on the Bethlehem property, and dedicated on the second Sunday after Epiphany, 1891. Teacher G. Schaefer, from California, was called to teach the primary classes and was installed on the first Sunday after Epiphany, but resigned in October, 1893, to accept a call to Milwaukee, Wis. He was succeeded by Teacher C. Niewedde in April, 1895; but at the termination of the school-year 1896 he was transferred to St. Paul's Station. During the prolonged vacancy Missionaries Kossmann and F. W. Wenzel taught in the primary department. On the second Sunday in September, 1902, Mr. Geo. P. Wolf, a graduate from the Teachers' Seminary, Addison, was placed in charge of the school, but remained only a short time. He was succeeded by another graduate from that institution, Theo. Wilder, who on the 22d Sunday after Trinity, 1906, entered upon his work. After a year in Bethlehem School, and another in St. Paul's School, he resigned. He was succeeded on the first Sunday in September, 1908, by the Addison graduate J. Bruns, whose stay was brief. Mr. F. J. Odendahl, who had been superintendent of the Sunday-school in "Sailors' Home" when Rev. Doescher served our mission there, was for a number of years teacher of the primary classes. Mr. L. Palm, an Addison graduate, taught in Bethlehem from September 5, 1909, to April, 1912. Rev. Kramer frequently assisted in the school work. The present force of teachers consists of Napoleon Seeberry, transferred from St. Paul's in 1910, W. Schrieber, transferred from Napoleonville, La., 1911, L. Pollert, Addison graduate, since September, 1912, and Teacher C. F. Lange, since April, 1912. In the summer of 1913, another class-room was added to the school. The vestry room of the chapel had previously been enlarged and, like St. Paul's Station, the school now has four flourishing classes.

MANSURA, LA.

St. Paul's.

Mansura, Avoyelles Parish, is a village 165 miles northwest of New Orleans. About 2½ miles north of the village is a colored Creole settlement called Cocoville. Mr. Henry Thomas, a member of St. Paul's Church, New Orleans, came to this community in search of work, and began to tell the people about his Lutheran church and school in New Orleans. The result of Henry's missionary work was the visit of Revs. Lankenau and Siebelitz from

ST. PAUL'S CHAPEL, MANSURA.

New Orleans. In March, 1899, Rev. Lankenau held the first Lutheran service in Mansura, in Scott Normand's house. A chapel costing $400 was built and dedicated on Pentecost Sunday, 1899. The first resident missionary was W. Pretzsch, a St. Louis graduate, who was inducted into his office October 8, 1899. In the spring of 1901, he resigned on account of the climate. During his time a small parsonage was built. He was succeeded on the 13th Sunday after Trinity, the same year, by Rev. Martin Weinhold, a graduate of St. Louis. In the beginning of the year 1905, however, sickness compelled him to resign. In April of the same year

REV. W. PRETZSCH.   REV. M. WEINHOLD.   REV. CHAS. D. PEAY.

Rev. F. W. Wenzel was transferred from New Orleans to Mansura and served the congregation until he accepted a pastorate in Wisconsin in the summer of 1908. During the vacancy of two years St. Paul's was supplied by Rev. Ed. H. Schmidt of Napoleonville, La. The Luther College students C. P. Thompson and Eugene Berger taught school there. Pastors K. Kretzschmar and J. Kossmann were temporarily in charge of the church. The present pastor, Chas. D. Peay, was transferred from Monroe, N. C., to Mansura in 1910, and was inducted into his office by Rev. Schmidt June 26.

NAPOLEONVILLE, LA.

Napoleonville, Assumption Parish, is situated in the southeastern part of Louisiana, about 60 miles due west of New Orleans. A colored citizen of that town moved to New Orleans and became

REV. EUG. R. BERGER.   TEACHER F. EBERHARD.

a member of St. Paul's Church. His name was Joseph Nelson. Losing his position in that city, he returned to his former home and, like Henry Thomas in Mansura, began to testify of his Savior to his people and to tell them about the Lutheran Church. At his request Rev. Lankenau came to Napoleonville, and in June, 1905, preached the first Lutheran sermon to the people of that town. On November 5, of the following year, Teacher Gehner, transferred from Bethlehem, New Orleans, opened a Lutheran school in a rented hall. He resigned in 1907, and F. W. Eberhard, an Addison graduate, took charge of the school October 13, of that year, and taught it for three years. The Mission Board called Rev. Ed. H. Schmidt, of Seymour, Ind., a St. Louis graduate, to the field, and he entered upon his work in May, 1908. In the same year a chapel and school under one roof was built, which was dedicated the Sunday after Easter by Rev. Kramer and Prof.

CHAPEL AT NAPOLEONVILLE, LA.

Mueller, of New Orleans. The Addison graduate W. Schrieber taught the school from September, 1910, till the end of the school-year, 1911. Missionaries K. Kretzschmar, Kramer, and Prof. Mueller were temporarily in charge of the mission. Since his ordination on the first Sunday in July, 1911, Rev. Eugene R. Berger is the missionary in Napoleonville. No congregation has been organized.

JUNIOR LUTHERAN ORCHESTRA, NAPOLEONVILLE, LA.

NEW MISSION FIELDS IN NEW ORLEANS, LA.

1. Trinity Chapel.

On Elmira Street, in the third district of the city, Rev. Ed. H. Schmidt began mission work in the beginning of the year 1912. A few children were gathered into the Sunday-school. In the fall of the same year Student Paul Lehman, of Luther College, opened a Lutheran school in a rented hall. Rev. Schmidt conducted services there on Sunday afternoons, and a class of 6 adults

TEACHER PETER ROBINSON AND PUPILS OF TRINITY SCHOOL, NEW ORLEANS.

has been confirmed. For a few months in the fall of 1913, Miss Adeline Winn, a graduate of Luther College, was in charge of the school. Upon her removal Mr. Peter Robinson, who was educated in St. Paul's Church from childhood, was prevailed upon to take her place.

2. Carrollton Station.

The mission work in Carrollton, abandoned in 1894 as hopeless, has been resumed by Rev. Kramer. During the summer vacation 1912, Teacher Napoleon Seeberry conducted the school in an old lodge hall with success. Miss Eleanore King, a graduate

HALL AND SCHOOL IN CARROLLTON.

of Luther College, opened the school in September with an increased enrollment. Two members formerly belonging to the old "Rooster Church" attend Rev. Kramer's services in the afternoon on Sundays. Hopes are entertained of gathering a congregation again through the flourishing school.

REDEEMER SCHOOL, NEW ORLEANS.

3. Redeemer.

Towards the end of the year 1912 the professors of Luther College, R. A. Wilde and H. Meibohm, decided to begin a Lutheran mission in the vicinity of Dupré Street, about two miles from St. Paul's. A private dwelling was rented and equipped with old school desks. With a few children Miss Sophie Raymond opened a school, which is steadily increasing. Prof. Meibohm conducts regular services every Sunday night, and Prof. Wilde supervises the Sunday-school.

4. St. John's.

This station is under the care of Rev. A. O. Friedrich and Mount Zion Church. In February, 1913, Student C. Stoll, from Concordia Seminary, St. Louis, opened a school in a small house, the rent of which is paid by Mount Zion. In November he went to Immanuel College to complete his theological studies, and Miss Adeline Winn, who had taught at St. Paul's and Trinity Chapel, succeeded him. Rev. Friedrich preaches on Sunday afternoons.

MISS ADELINE WINN, Teacher.

VIRGINIA.

Beginning of the Mission.

Towards the end of the year 1880, Rev. W. R. Buehler came to Prince Edward Co., Va., where his wife had bought a farm. Rev. Buehler for years had been a missionary in Africa, but his health failing, he came to the United States. He located in the salubrious climate of Virginia to recuperate. The colored people of the community requested him to preach to them and to instruct their children. He wrote to the Mission Board and offered his services. Having passed a satisfactory examination before a committee, a call was extended to him to serve the

Colored Mission. His wife donated the grounds to the mission, and a log schoolhouse was built. Here Rev. Buehler preached and taught school, but it was not a success. The section near the village Meherrin, five miles distant, seemed more favorable for mission work, and the log house was transported to the new field. The labor here was not in vain. Though Rev. Buehler, in common with other white pioneer missionaries, had to suffer from the prejudices of both races, he succeeded in baptizing and confirming a few. In 1886, he left Virginia with the purpose of returning to Germany. During his sojourn in New York he was called to be assistant pastor of Rev. Halfmann's congregation. He died in the smallpox hospital there in 1887.

St. Matthew's, Meherrin.

When the Rev. Buehler severed his connection with the mission in Virginia, the Synodical Conference, in 1886, at the suggestion of the Board, resolved to abandon the field and to advise

REV. W. R. BUEHLER.   REV. D. H. SCHOOFF.   REV. E. POLZIN.

the eight communicant members to move to Little Rock or to New Orleans, where there were Lutheran churches and schools. But they refused to do this. They preferred to gather with their children in the log schoolhouse on Sundays and conduct devotional exercises according to Lutheran practice. Occasionally Rev. C. J. Oehlschlaeger, of Richmond, visited them and administered to them the means of grace. At their request he frequently petitioned the Mission Board to send them another missionary. The Board decided to give Meherrin another trial and sent Student

Hoernicke, from Springfield, to supply the station temporarily. Moved by the faithful adherence of these members to the Lutheran Church, the Synodical Conference, in 1888, resolved to resume the work, and empowered the Board to call a missionary. Meanwhile theological students from Springfield, D. H. Schooff, Alfred Brauer, and F. J. Lankenau, acted as supplies. Their reports were promising. The little flock increased. In 1890, the Springfield graduate D. H. Schooff accepted the call of the Board. He was ordained by Rev. Oehlschlaeger in Richmond, Va., on the

ST. MATTHEW'S CHAPEL AND PARSONAGE, MEHERRIN, VA.

14th Sunday after Trinity, in 1890, and a few days later he was introduced to his people at Meherrin. During the long vacancy the congregation had increased from 8 to 34 communicant members. In 1892, a combined church and school was built and dedicated September 6. A parsonage was also erected, the first of its kind in the Colored Mission. Rev. Schooff served the mission in Meherrin faithfully for seventeen years. Chiefly on account of his family he resigned in October, 1907. Prof. M. Lochner, of Immanuel College, served the congregation during the vacancy till May, 1912. Rev. Emil H. Polzin, the present missionary, took charge of the station May 12, of that year. — The preaching places Bruceville and Pleasant Grove have been abandoned.

YONKERS, NEW YORK.

Bethany.

During the years 1890—1895 several Lutherans moved from Meherrin, Va., to New York, particularly to Yonkers, where they found employment as domestics in wealthy families. The emigration continued till there was a considerable colored Lutheran colony in Yonkers. They petitioned Rev. A. von Schlichten to serve them with the means of grace, which he did. The Mission Board was repeatedly requested to provide this mission with a missionary, but it was unable to comply with the request, and for a time the services were discontinued. In 1907, however, Rev. von Schlichten resumed the work, as there were at that time some 40 colored Lutherans from Meherrin residing in Yonkers. July 8, 1910, he organized, with 8 communicant members, the Ev. Luth. Bethany Congregation. On account of increasing work in his own church, which demanded his entire time, and owing to the danger which threatened the colored Lutherans from proselytizing sectarians, a missionary in Yonkers had become an imperative necessity. In 1911, the Mission Board called William O. Hill, a graduate of Immanuel College, who after his graduation had assisted Rev. McDavid in Charlotte, N. C. He was ordained by the writer in Grace Church, Greensboro, March 5, 1911, and entered upon his missionary work in Yonkers a week later. The German Lutheran church placed its parish house at the disposal of the colored congregation, where it has a commodious and convenient house of worship.

REV. W. O. HILL.

SPRINGFIELD, ILL.

Holy Trinity.

At the request of some colored people Rev. Prof. H. Wyneken, with the assistance of the theological students, began mission work in a small and quiet way in Springfield, in 1882. His labor was not in vain. Toward the end of the year 1887, the Board assumed control of the mission, under the condition, however, that the Professor should direct it until a missionary could be secured. On March 11, 1888, the first catechumen class and the Ev. Luth. Holy Trinity Church were organized. The services were generally conducted in the auditorium of the Seminary. A graduate of the

HOLY TRINITY CHURCH, SPRINGFIELD, ILL.

Seminary, H. S. Knabenschuh, was the first resident missionary. He was ordained and introduced into his work September 23, 1888, by the chairman of the Mission Board, Rev. Sapper. A beautiful chapel and school combined was built at the cost of $4,000. It was set apart for the service of God February 24, 1889. Rev. Knabenschuh resigned in February, 1893. During the vacancy Prof. J. Herzer was in charge of the mission. From August, 1894, to March, 1895, Rev. F. Herm. Meyer served the church. A mis-understanding between him and the congregation necessitated his removal to the North Carolina field. A vacancy of nearly eight years followed, during which Prof. Herzer, with the assistance of Prof. L. Wessel and students, served the congregation. In the

PROF. H. WYNEKEN.

PROF. J. HERZER.

PROF. L. WESSEL.

PROF. O. C. A. BOECLER.

fall of 1902, Rev. Lucius Thalley, colored, a Springfield graduate, who had been ordained in Charlotte, N. C., by the writer, was placed in charge of the mission.

In the latter part of 1905, Rev. Thalley retired on account of failing health, going to Colorado, where he still resides. Again Prof. Herzer acted as supply until Rev. James H. Doswell, of Gold Hill, N. C., was transferred to Springfield by the Board in

January, 1907. In the fall, two years later, Rev. Doswell was called to take charge of the mission in St. Louis, and Prof. O. C. A. Boecler, with the help of students, has since served the congregation. Student John McDavid of Bethlehem station, New Orleans, who in 1892 entered the Springfield Seminary to prepare himself for the ministry, was in 1896 placed in charge of the school and taught it until November, 1904, when he was transferred to the St. Louis Mission. The parsonage was built by him.

REV. L. THALLEY.

ST. LOUIS.

Grace Church.

For years the Mission Board had been contemplating a mission among the 45,000 negroes in St. Louis. Tentatively a colored student from Springfield, by the name of Thompson, was requested

REV. J. DOSWELL.

MRS. M. BAEHLER.

to begin missionary work among his people in that city. But his work was not encouraging. In November, 1903, Rev. L. Thalley, of Springfield, delivered his first sermon to a good-sized audience, and continued the services until on account of sickness he retired. Student McDavid assisted him in the Sunday-school work. On November 16, 1904, he opened a Lutheran school and presided over it until the summer of 1905, when the Board called him to Charlotte, N. C. A catechumen class, 8 adults, which he gathered and instructed, was confirmed by Prof. Herzer on the 3d Sunday after Trinity, and 10 were received by baptism. After McDavid's removal the work was continued by students of Concordia Seminary. These are also doing active missionary work in the St. Louis County Infirmary. The frequent changes in the missionary force were detrimental to the progress of the mission, and in March, 1908, the Board decided to discontinue it. But the Lutheran negroes do not so easily give up their Lutheran Church which they

GRACE CHURCH AND SCHOOL, ST. LOUIS.

have learned to love, as the history of Little Rock, Meherrin, and other places shows. The petition of the members of Grace Church for Lutheran services and school was granted by the Board, and it transferred Missionary Doswell from Springfield to St. Louis. On March 30, 1909, he took charge of the mission, and in September of the same year he opened a school. The work made slow progress. In November, 1913, the missionary's labors were interrupted by sickness, and the station is temporarily supplied by Rev. J. E. Tice, who is an applicant for missionary work in the Lutheran Church. A member of one of the local Lutheran churches, Mrs. Baehler, has always worked faithfully and zealously for the mission, particularly during vacancies.

NORTH CAROLINA.

The Alpha Synod.

There were colored Lutherans in the South before the Civil War. Lutheran slaveholders provided for the spiritual wants of their slaves. On the galleries of the churches places were set apart for the slaves, and the white pastors instructed them in God's Word preparatory to Baptism and Confirmation. They were also admitted to the Lord's Supper. With the emancipation of the slaves in 1863, this spiritual provision ceased. Only a few remained faithful to the Lutheran Church. There were preachers also posing as Lutherans, but who, as most of the colored preachers at the time, were illiterate and possessed no knowledge of true Christianity nor of confessional Lutheranism. The first Lutheran preacher in North Carolina was Michael Coble, who, at a revival meeting, was converted to Methodism. In the year 1888, the North Carolina Synod of the Lutheran Church resolved to begin a mission among the colored people. In that year four colored men were ordained to the office of holy ministry by pastors of that Synod. These

REV. D. KOONTS.

men had been preaching for years and were known as Lutherans. They were advised to organize their own Synod, which they did. Together with some laymen they met, at the beginning of the year 1890, in Cabarrus Co., N. C., and organized the Alpha Synod. The officers elected were — David Koonts, president, and W. Philo Phifer, secretary, he being the only one who had learned to read and write. None of these men, not even the president, was able to recite from memory the text of Luther's Small Catechism. They conducted divine services in four communities, generally in public schoolhouses, and any one that acknowledged the presence of the body and blood of Christ in the Lord's Supper was regarded a Lutheran and confirmed. A few

4

such Lutherans were found in the communities where preaching-places were established. No congregations were organized. Shortly after the adjournment of the Synod President Koonts died, and the Alpha Synod died with him. At the beginning of 1891, Rev. Phifer wrote in the name of his colleagues, Sam. Holt and Nathan Clap, to Dr. Schwan, President of the Missouri Synod, asking for help. He transmitted the letter to the Mission Board, which requested Missionaries Burgdorf, Schooff, and the writer to investigate the North Carolina mission field.

Beginning of the Mission.

The committee appointed by the Board to investigate the North Carolina mission field held a conference with the preachers

GRACE SCHOOL, CONCORD, N. C.

Phifer, Holt, and Clap in a negro cabin at Burlington, the proprietor of the only hotel in the place having turned them out because they were negro missionaries. Easy catechetical questions were put to these preachers, but only a few were correctly answered. The theological examination was not satisfactory to the committee, but it saw in the field a door which the Lord had opened, hoped that the preachers in course of time might be utilized, and advised the Board to take charge of the field, provided a man could be found who would instruct the preachers and superintend the mission. With the consent of his congregations in New Orleans, the writer in August, 1891, was transferred to

GRACE CHURCH, CONCORD, N. C.

North Carolina. In September he arrived with his family at Concord, where he soon learned to realize more than ever what it means to be a missionary among the colored people of the South. On the 17th Sunday after Trinity he was introduced at a service conducted by Rev. Phifer in an old store-room. His text was Acts 20, 29: "For I know this, that after my departing shall grievous wolves enter in among you, not sparing the flock." The words were not very comforting from the mouth of his predecessor, but, fortunately for the new missionary, Phifer, as is often the case

TEACHER E. F. ROLF.

with colored preachers, did not enter into any explanation of the text.

As the old store-room was both dilapidated and too small, steps were taken to erect a new church. It was dedicated July 2, 1893. The missionary also opened a school, which he taught till Christmas, 1892, when Teacher E. F. Rolf, an Addison graduate, took charge of it. With ability and fidelity he conducted the school for seven years. Out of consideration for the health of his wife he accepted a call to Seward, Nebr., in 1900.

Grace, Concord.

A petition addressed to the schoolchildren of the Synodical Conference by Rev. F. W. Herzberger, who on a visit to Concord convinced himself of the necessity of a new school-building, brought enough money to erect a two-story schoolhouse and enough to

REV. J. PH. SCHMIDT.

REV. C. H. MESSERLI.

spare for a chapel at Elon College. It was dedicated May 19, 1895, Prof. W. H. T. Dau delivering the address. In September, 1898, the writer was transferred to Charlotte, and Rev. J. Ph. Schmidt, who on the 14th of August, at the convention of the Synodical Conference in Cincinnati, O., was ordained by Rev. C. J. Otto Hanser, succeeded him. In January, 1909, the Mission Board called him to the chair of Theology at Immanuel College, Greensboro, but he continued to serve the Concord charge till the arrival of his successor, C. H. Messerli, a graduate of the Seminary in St. Louis. He was ordained September 12, of the same year, and resigned again in the fall of 1912 to accept a call to Edgerton, O. During the vacancy Prof. Schmidt served the congregation. On August 21, 1913, he installed the present pastor and missionary, Rev. W. G. Schwehn.

Three teachers have worked in the Concord school besides Mr. Rolf. The Addison graduate W. Lohrmann entered upon his office September 2, 1900, but after two years he resigned on account of sickness. He was followed by Teacher H. L. Persson, of Charlotte, in the fall of 1903. Mr. M. N. Carter, colored,

REV. W. G. SCHWEHN.   TEACHER W. LOHRMANN.   TEACHER H. L. PERSSON.

educated in the high school of Baltimore and at Capital University, Columbus, O., conducted the school from the beginning of 1906 to March, 1910. The Misses Mamie Persson and Wilmar Barnhardt have at various times assisted.

Immanuel Chapel, Cabarrus Co.

Eight miles northeast of Concord, in the country, at a place called Reimerstown, the writer began mission work in the fall of 1891. The services were conducted in an old schoolhouse. A chapel was built for $300 and dedicated September 11, 1892. On the same day the first class of adult catechumens was confirmed and Immanuel Congregation organized. Until 1901, this station was served from Concord. For a year Rev. Paul Engelbert was in charge of it. Since 1902, it has been served from Mount Pleasant. Missionaries J. Ph. Schmidt, Engelbert, St. Doswell, Rich. Oehlschlaeger, and the present pastor, Rev. John Alston,

IMMANUEL CHAPEL, CABARRUS CO., N. C.

have labored in this field, and students from Immanuel College have taught summer-school. Most of the colored people have moved away from this section, and the congregation is decreasing in members.

Mount Calvary, Mount Pleasant.

Nine miles east of Concord is Mount Pleasant. From this village a goodly number of people attended the services at Immanuel Chapel, Reimerstown. In the winter of 1893, they requested the writer, on account of the distance, seven miles, to preach to them at Mount Pleasant, which was done. For years the services were conducted in this or that public schoolhouse or in a private dwelling. The station was served from Concord till 1899. In that year Rev. Paul Engelbert took charge of it, and in 1900 organized the congregation, Mount Calvary. A year later the Mission Board bought an old public schoolhouse with an acre of land. The first resident pastor of Mount Pleasant was St. Doswell, a graduate of the Seminary in Springfield, who was ordained on the 15th Sunday after Trinity, 1902, by Rev. J. C. Schmidt

REV. ST. DOSWELL.   REV. J. ALSTON.

in Greensboro. He resided there till his death, July 9, 1908. His remains were brought to Meherrin, Va., his native town, for burial. He was succeeded by Rev. John Alston, a graduate of Immanuel College, who, together with his classmates Fred Foard and Chas. Peay, was ordained in Concord July 4, 1909, and a week later installed by Rev. J. Ph. Schmidt. The new chapel was dedicated April 24, 1910. A neat parsonage was built later.

MOUNT CALVARY CHAPEL AND PARSONAGE, MOUNT PLEASANT, N. C.

St. Peter's, Dry's Schoolhouse.

In the fall of the year 1897, a delegation from a colored settlement in the neighborhood of Dry's Schoolhouse, Cabarrus Co., seven miles south of Concord, came to attend the Lutheran services at Grace Church. On the previous Sunday the same delegation had paid a similar visit to the Presbyterian church of the city. They were in search of a pastor. The Baptists and Methodists were excluded from the list of eligible candidates. Shortly afterwards the delegation returned and requested the writer to come to Dry's Schoolhouse and preach to them. He complied with their

PETER AND CHAS. REID,
Members of St. Peter's Church.

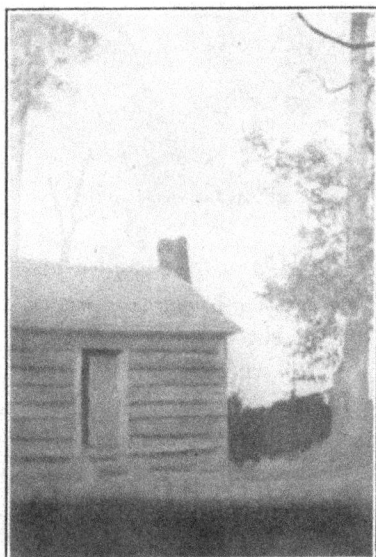

"HOLY OAK" AND OLD SCHOOL.

request. On the 9th Sunday after Trinity, 1898, after a year of preaching and catechetical instruction, he held services under a large oak tree, near the schoolhouse, and baptized 29, among them 8 adults, and confirmed 24. These organized themselves into a congregation, which bears the name of Ev. Luth. St. Peter's Chapel. The tree has been named the "Holy Oak," and still stands as a monument of the sacred act. The congregation bought 2½ acres of land, and with the help of the Mission Board erected a chapel, which was dedicated August 5, 1900. The congregation belonged to the Concord charge till the fall of 1902. From that time on it has been served from Mount Pleasant. The present pastor is Rev. John Alston.

Mount Calvary, Sandy Ridge.

About seven miles north of Concord is a colored settlement called Sandy Ridge. A Lutheran family which belonged to Grace Church in Concord moved to this settlement and called on Rev. J. Ph. Schmidt to come and administer the means of grace. The people gathered for services at the house of this Lutheran family.

MOUNT CALVARY CHAPEL, SANDY RIDGE.

On July 6, 1902, Rev. Schmidt organized the Mount Calvary Congregation of Sandy Ridge. Two acres of land were bought by the congregation, and with the help of the Mission Board a chapel was built, which was set apart for the service of God in July, 1905. This congregation is distinguished from the others of the Mission by maintaining a parochial school at its own expense. It belongs to the Concord charge. Rev. Schmidt served it till 1909, Rev. C. H. Messerli till 1912. For a year Prof. Schmidt, of Immanuel College,

THIRD-GENERATION LUTHERANS.

acted as supply. Since September, 1913, it has been under the pastoral care of Rev. W. G. Schwehn. Miss Addie McTier is the teacher.

Kannapolis.

Kannapolis is a modern progressive cotton factory town, three miles from Sandy Ridge. The small colored population has neither church nor school. In December, 1913, Rev. Schwehn, of Concord, began to hold services and Sunday-school in the house of a Lutheran. The president of the cotton mills, Mr. J. W. Cannon, has promised a building site for a Lutheran chapel.

Concordia, Rockwell, Rowan Co.

In the spring of 1893, the writer preached for the first time to the colored people of Rowan Co. in an old schoolhouse near Rockwell. Twenty-four men and women had signed a petition for Lutheran services, and at a meeting personally declared that they desired to be instructed by the writer in God's Word and Luther's doctrine, and to become members of the Lutheran Church. Among these signers was a married couple which during slavery days had been baptized by a Lutheran pastor. On Pentecost Sunday, 1894, he organized the Concordia Congregation and served it from Concord. Rev. F. Herm. Meyer, who resided in Salisbury, was in charge of it from September, 1895, till May, 1896. After his apostasy the congregation was again under the pastoral care of the writer. Ten stations at that time belonged to his charge. With the exception of Lexington all the churches which had been served by Meyer remained faithful to the Lutheran Church. The Concordia Chapel was dedicated July 15, 1897. In the

REV. P. ENGELBERT.

same year, on the 9th Sunday after Trinity, Rev. Geo. Schutes assumed the pastorate. He was succeeded by Rev. P. Engelbert, a graduate of the St. Louis Seminary, from September, 1899, to 1903. Then Rev. Schutes acted as supply for a year. The Springfield graduate James H. Doswell, colored, was ordained in Rockwell on the 16th Sunday after Trinity and remained till January, 1907, when he was transferred to Springfield, Ill. Rev. W. H. Lash, of Salisbury, was pastor during the vacancy. The present missionary is Rev. F. Foard who entered upon his office July 16, 1909. Rockwell forms a pastorate together with Gold Hill, Mount Zion, and Albemarle. The missionary resides at Gold Hill.

Zion, Gold Hill.

In the summer of 1893, a delegation from Gold Hill came to Rockwell, where the writer had established a Lutheran mission, and presented to him a petition signed by 50 men and women to come and preach at Gold Hill. That mining town is twenty miles from Concord and four miles from Rockwell. The first house of worship was, as usually, the old negro schoolhouse. The doors of the school being closed against us by a hostile school board,

ZION CHAPEL, GOLD HILL, N. C.

REV. F. FOARD.

we found temporary refuge in an abandoned negro cabin. There, in March, 1894, Zion Ev. Luth. Church was organized. Rev. F. Herm. Meyer was pastor of the congregation from August, 1895, to May, 1896. On the 9th Sunday after Trinity, 1897, Zion Chapel was dedicated, and Rev. Geo. Schutes was introduced as pastor of Gold Hill and Rockwell. The history of these two stations is almost identical, as they have always belonged to the same pastorate, with the exception that Rev. James Doswell resided in Gold Hill, and that his cousin, St. Doswell, acted as supply for a time after his removal to Springfield. Missionaries Engelbert, Doswell, and Foard have conducted the school.

Albemarle, Stanly Co.

Albemarle, the county seat of Stanly Co., is thirty miles southeast of Salisbury and fifteen miles from Gold Hill. It is a new field and is served by Rev. Fred Foard, who opened school there in a private house in October, 1911. He preaches there once a month. The mission possesses no property in Albemarle, and no congregation has been organized.

SCHOOL AND CHURCH, ALBEMARLE, N. C.

St. John's, Salisbury.

A woman residing in Salisbury, who on her visits to relatives at Gold Hill attended the Lutheran services there, requested the writer to give her catechetical instruction, which he occasionally did. This was the beginning of the Salisbury mission. In the

SCHOOL, SALISBURY, N. C.

fall of 1895, Rev. F. H. Meyer, who had returned from Springfield to North Carolina, opened a Lutheran school in a rented dwelling. When, a year later, he renounced the Lutheran faith and went over to the Baptists, Student Theo. Volkert, from the Springfield Seminary, who had for a year been doing supply work in Greensboro, succeeded him for a few months in the school. The writer continued the work till the arrival of the new missionary, Rev. G. Schutes, a St. Louis graduate, who was ordained

REV. W. H. LASH.

REV. G. SCHUTES.

TEACHER J. F. M. THALLEY.

in Concord on the 8th Sunday after Trinity. The Mission Board acquired a suitable building site, and a chapel was erected and dedicated February 19, 1899. On the 17th Sunday after Trinity, 1904, Rev. Schutes delivered his valedictory sermon, and on the same day ordained and introduced his successor, W. H. Lash, a Springfield graduate. A tornado that swept over Salisbury

St. John's Chapel, Salisbury, N.C.

April 5, 1905, completely destroyed the chapel, and for two years Rev. Lash conducted services and school in a lodge hall. The new chapel was dedicated September 15, 1907, and Miss Elizah Johnston, a graduate of Immanuel College, took charge of the school and taught it till the beginning of the year 1909. An abandoned Methodist chapel, built of undressed lumber, 50 feet away from the Lutheran chapel, was purchased by the Board and converted into a school-room. In September, 1913, Teacher J. F. W. Thalley, who had studied at Springfield for several years, was called to assist Rev. Lash in the school.

Conover and Catawba, Catawba Co.

The writer was for a time the only clerical representative of the Synodical Conference in the Carolinas. Naturally he looked and longed for brethren with whom he could associate. When, therefore, Rev. Prof. Dau and others came to Conover, he joined

MOUNT OLIVE CHAPEL, CATAWBA, N. C.

himself to them. On his occasional visits he was frequently requested by colored people of the village to preach to them. A petition, signed by thirty men and women to that effect, was also sent him. St. John's Ev. Luth. Church, of which Prof. Dau was the pastor, without any solicitations offered its house of worship for services to the colored people. This offer, coming from a Southern white congregation, was highly appreciated. This sentiment will be better understood when it is considered that five colored communicant members, who have been Lutherans "from befo' de war," belonged to this congregation. On Epiphany Sunday, 1895, the writer preached to the colored people in St. John's. Later a lady of Concordia congregation placed a commodious house

PROF. W. H. T. DAU.

at the disposal of the missionary, and two students of Concordia College conducted the Sunday-school in his absence. Prof. Dau and the other professors, who were frequently called on to help the missionaries, supported the cause of the mission in word and deed. But because most of the members resided in the neighborhood of Catawba, it was deemed advisable to permanently locate there. With the help of the white Lutheran churches in Catawba Co. an acre of land was purchased, and with the assistance of the Mission Board a chapel was built. It was dedicated on the 16th Sunday after Trinity, 1902. The small chapel at Conover was set apart for the service of God, August 25, 1907. Both congregations are small and belong to the Salisbury charge. Besides the writer Missionaries Meyer and Schutes have served them. Since 1904, they are under the pastoral care of Rev. Lash.

Mount Zion, The Rocks, Rowan Co.

At the beginning of the year 1904, a few Lutheran families living quite a distance from the Concordia Church at Rockwell were dismissed from the congregation for the purpose of organizing themselves into a congregation of their own. Rev. Geo. Schutes ministered to their spiritual wants till he resigned in 1904. The services were temporarily conducted in the house of a member. In the course of time the members bought a piece of land and began the erection of a chapel. As the work was done by the members, the building made slow progress. The cost amounted to $650, of which $75 was contributed by outside friends. It was ready for dedication on the third Sunday in November, 1908. From 1904 to 1909, Mount Zion belonged to the Salisbury charge and was served by Rev. Lash. In that year Rev. Fred Foard assumed the pastorate and is still serving this congregation. The

MOUNT ZION CHAPEL, THE ROCKS, N. C.

congregation is blessed with children, and religious instruction is given them for two months in the summer by a female teacher or by students of Immanuel College.

St. Paul's, Charlotte.

At the time the Mission Board, in 1891, took charge of the North Carolina mission field, there were two colored Lutherans in Charlotte, Rev. W. P. Phifer and his wife. During the first two years after his arrival the writer preached once a month in Charlotte and gave catechetical instruction to Rev. Phifer. Two congregations of the North Carolina Synod donated to the mission two small lots, on which a chapel for $900 was built. On the 18th Sunday after Trinity, 1892, it was dedicated. Prof. W. H. T. Dau delivered the dedicatory sermon. From September, 1898, to July, 1903, the writer was in charge of the station, and Rev. Phifer devoted his time chiefly to school work. The first and only division in any of our colored congregations occurred in Charlotte in the year 1900. Rev. Phifer being the only available man, he was requested by the Board to serve some country congregations in Cabarrus Co. He declined to move to the country and teach school. He sent his resignation to the Board, and established an opposition church, persuading the majority of the members to follow him. Within a year and a half all his members had left

5

ST. PAUL'S CHURCH AND SCHOOL, CHARLOTTE, N. C.

him. He was then received into the Ohio Synod, which stationed
him at Baltimore, where he died in 1911.

In the fall of 1900, the Mission Board transferred Teacher
H. L. Persson from Southern Pines to Charlotte. As the writer
was called by the Board to take initial steps towards the establishment of a preparatory school for the education of colored ministers

REV. JOHN McDAVID.

TEACHER FRANK ALSTON.

and teachers, Rev. Theo. Buch, of Southern Pines, succeeded him. He terminated his missionary activity in the spring of 1905 by accepting a call to a white congregation. Later he severed his connection with the Missouri Synod and joined the General Council. The colored teacher, E. W. Reid, who had studied several years at the institutions at Springfield, Ill., and New Ulm, Minn., succeeded Mr. Persson in the fall of 1903, but resigned temporarily at the end of the school-year, 1906. In the year 1905, the Board called the missionary teacher John McDavid, who for years had been working in the missions at Springfield and St. Louis, both as teacher and missionary, to Charlotte. He was ordained by the writer in the presence of his congregation on the 5th Sunday after Trinity. Student John Alston and the ministerial candidate Willie O. Hill have alternately assisted him in the school. On March 7, 1909, Teacher Frank Alston, the first graduate from the Teachers' Course of Immanuel College, was called to the Charlotte school as Rev. McDavid's assistant.

Mount Zion, Meyersville, Mecklenburg Co.

In 1896, at the beginning of the year, the writer and his assistant, Rev. Phifer, began mission work on Mr. J. S. Meyer's large plantation near Charlotte. About 100 men and women were either day laborers or "croppers" on his land. Most of them were churchless. In rainy weather the services and the Sunday-school were conducted in the home of Mr. Poe, in fair weather under the large trees near the house. Mr. Meyer was favorably disposed to the mission and offered a building lot, 100 feet square, for $50, which offer was accepted. A friend of the Colored Mission in Wisconsin donated $250 for a chapel, which was dedicated March 21, 1897, and bears the name of Mount Zion. The entire plantation is now the finest suburb of Charlotte. Beautiful residences with all modern conveniences have been erected on the grounds where the negro log cabins once stood. The mission property has, therefore, also become very valuable. Rev. Phifer succeeded in prejudicing this congregation also against the white missionary. After a few months, however, most of the members returned and apologized. The congregation has always been served by missionaries located in Charlotte. The present pastor is Rev. McDavid.

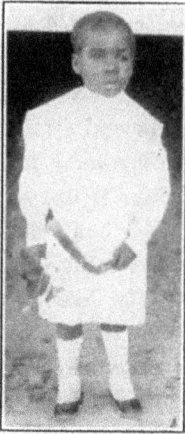

"McDavid's Lamb."

Mount Zion Chapel, Meyersville, N. C.

St. James, Southern Pines.

Southern Pines, Moore Co., 105 miles southeast of Charlotte, is a winter resort, particularly for tuberculous people. Two Lutheran families of Gold Hill which had moved to Southern Pines requested the writer in the first part of the year 1898 to come and preach to them. In September of the same year the Board transferred Teacher H. L. Persson from Greensboro to this place to establish a Lutheran school. As elsewhere in pioneer days of the mission, so also here the services and the school were conducted

ST. JAMES CHAPEL, SOUTHERN PINES, N. C.

in old schoolhouses or in a private dwelling. The native white people did not look favorably upon the missionaries and their work. The teacher especially was the target of abusive tongues. The work of the Lord made progress nevertheless. On the Sunday after Easter 1899, St. James Congregation was organized. In the same year, by the generosity of the Holy Cross Church of Saginaw, Mich., Rev. H. Speckhard, pastor, who has always taken a hearty interest in our Colored Mission, a handsome chapel, at the cost of $300, was erected. It was dedicated August 5, 1900, and on the same day Rev. M. Nickel, the successor of the writer, who had been ordained by his brother in Akron, O., July 29, was

REV. H. SPECKHARD.

REV. C. R. MARCH.

inducted into his office. On account of his health he resigned a year later. On the 13th Sunday after Trinity, 1901, he was succeeded by Rev. Theo. Buch and after his removal to Charlotte, in the summer of 1903, Rev. H. Essig took his place. He served the station for about nine months, from the 13th Sunday after Trinity till the summer of 1904, when he resigned. From that time on missionaries from Charlotte served the congregation. In 1911, the Mission Board called Carrington R. March, a graduate of Immanuel College, to Southern Pines. He was ordained there July 16, by Rev. McDavid.

Bethlehem, Monroe, Union Co.

The Rev. Samuel W. Hampton, an old negro preacher, was instrumental in bringing the Lutheran mission into Monroe, a town situated about 25 miles southeast of Charlotte. In the beginning

HAMPTON CHAPEL, MONROE, N. C.

of the year 1900, he asked the writer to come to Monroe and establish a Lutheran mission in New Town, where he lived. Hampton owned, besides his house, an old schoolhouse, where he instructed a few children for a small tuition fee. This he placed at the disposal of the missionary. Later he donated this property to the Mission Board. On Palm Sunday, 1902, the writer baptized and confirmed 27 persons and organized Bethlehem Ev. Luth. Congregation. On a beautiful, centrally located plot of ground a chapel was built and dedicated June 7, 1903. Rev. Hampton was carried on his sick-bed on a cot to the chapel that he might attend the dedicatory services. Twenty days thereafter he died. In the fall of the same year Rev. H. Essig assumed charge of the station in connection with Southern Pines. He was succeeded for a short time by Yuku Mohamed, the alleged African prince, who was removed for cause. In 1909, the Mission Board called Rev. Charles D. Peay, a Greensboro graduate, to Monroe. He was ordained July 4, at Concord and installed a week later. Since his removal to Mansura, La., in 1910, the station has been

BETHLEHEM CHAPEL, MONROE, N. C.

under the pastoral care of Missionaries McDavid and Thompson in Charlotte. On account of the nomadic tendencies of the people the congregation has materially decreased.

Bethel, Greenville.

Greenville is a suburb in the northwestern part of Charlotte and is settled almost exclusively by colored people who have purchased or are purchasing homes through the Building and Loan Association. On September 4, 1911, Rev. McDavid opened a school in a small Methodist chapel. April 11, 1912, he organized Bethel Ev. Luth. Congregation with members who had formerly belonged to St. Paul's Church, and a few others. The Mission Board acquired two building lots, and with the help of some laborers Missionaries McDavid and Thompson and Prof. Alston erected, during vacation, a commodious brick chapel. The dedicatory services were

REV. C. P. THOMPSON.   BETHEL CHAPEL, GREENVILLE, N. C.

held August 4, 1912. The station is at present in charge of Rev. C. P. Thompson, who also conducts the school. Rev. Thompson received his education at Luther College, New Orleans, La. He was ordained by Rev. Alb. Witt in St. Paul's Church on July 17, 1910. For a short time he was missionary at Merigold, Miss. As this field did not come up to expectations, the Mission Board in March, 1911, transferred him to Charlotte.

Trinity, Elon College.

In Alamance Co. the writer found two preaching places, Springdale, or Holt's Chapel, and Elon College schoolhouse, which were poorly served by the colored preachers, Samuel Holt and Nathan Clap. For a year the writer preached once a month in this county, and then, being fully convinced of the deficiencies of these preachers to administer the means of grace to their hearers, persuaded them to resign. In 1893, the Mission Board called the St. Louis graduate F. Herm. Meyer to this field. He was ordained in Concord on the 7th Sunday after Trinity and inducted into his office at the schoolhouse, near Elon College, the following Sunday. He resided in Greensboro and preached there also in a lodge hall. A year later he was transferred to Springfield, Ill., and the Board called a graduate of that Seminary, John C. Schmidt, to succeed him. He was ordained in that old schoolhouse on July 29, 1894, and on the same day Rev. Meyer delivered his valedictory sermon. A chapel at the cost of $600 was built in the village in 1895, and dedicated in May of the same year. The two Lutheran families who lived at Springdale moved to Elon College, and as there was no material for missionary work, Holt's Chapel was abandoned. Rev. Samuel Holt died April 2, 1914. Trinity, Elon College, has always been served from Greensboro. Rev. Schmidt was in charge

TRINITY CHAPEL, ELON COLLEGE, N. C.

REV. SAMUEL HOLT.

of it till 1907, the writer till 1909, and Prof. Lochner till 1912. From that time on it has been served by Rev. O. R. Lynn. Several members have moved away, and the congregation is small.

Grace Church, Greensboro.

On his missionary journeys to Alamance Co. during the years 1891—1893, the writer explored Greensboro also, and found two adults who claimed to be Lutherans. Rev. Meyer was advised to reside in Greensboro and to establish a mission there. Seven souls were the fruit of his year's work. In 1894, Rev. John C. Schmidt began his work in the lodge hall at Greensboro, and on

GRACE CHURCH, GREENSBORO, N. C.

the last Sunday in Advent of the following year he had the pleasure
of organizing Grace Ev. Luth. Church with 8 communicants and
a few baptized children. On May 2, 1897, the little congregation
celebrated the dedication of its new handsome church and school.
Students from the Springfield Seminary assisted in the school
work until the Addison graduate Henry L. Persson, in August,

REV. J. C. SCHMIDT. TEACHER E. BUNTROCK. MRS. J. M. McCONNELL.

1897, took charge. Upon his removal to Southern Pines a year later, he was succeeded by E. A. H. Buntrock from the Teachers' Seminary in Addison. At the Synodical Conference in Cincinnati, O., 1898, he was commissioned by the Rev. Otto Hanser, who at the same time ordained Rev. J. Ph. Schmidt. After thirteen years of successful missionary activity in Greensboro, Rev. J. C. Schmidt resigned to accept a call to Pittsburg, Pa. For five years Rev. Prof. Wahlers of Immanuel College supplied the station. On September 1, 1912, the Immanuel College graduate Otho Lynn was called to the Greensboro pastorate. Miss Claudia Galloway is assistant in the school.

St. Luke's, High Point, Guilford Co.

High Point, fifteen miles south of Greensboro, is a manufacturing city where colored men find employment at living wages. Some Lutheran families, especially from Mount Pleasant, were attracted and moved to this city. The writer gathered these people into a congregation and served them from Greensboro from 1908 to 1911. After the writer's departure from North Carolina, Prof. Schmidt, of Immanuel College, ministered to their spiritual wants. The services were sometimes held in a hall, at other times in the house of a member. Since September, 1912, Rev. Otho Lynn, of Greensboro, serves High Point twice a month.

Winston-Salem, N. C.

Winston-Salem, 29 miles west of Greensboro, is a tobacco manufacturing center. The colored people are employed in the factories. It is a city of 29,000 inhabitants, with a large colored population. In his time Rev. J. C. Schmidt paid several missionary visits to this city. On September 3, 1899, he inducted Rev. J. F. Pfeiffer into his missionary work. He remained

REV. OTHO R. LYNN.

six months. Student E. E. Stueckert took his place for a season. He, in turn, was succeeded by Rev. Rich. Oehlschlaeger, who began his work on the 9th Sunday after Trinity and remained one year, when the work was abandoned. Hearing of some Lutheran families that had moved to Winston, the writer, in company with Rev. Lynn, called on them, November 19, 1913, made arrangements for regular services, and advised the Mission Board to give that promising field another chance. Rev. Otho Lynn, with the help of the theological students from Greensboro, is in charge of the station.

Fayetteville.

Fayetteville, Cumberland Co., is situated on Cape Fear River, fifty miles from Southern Pines. A silk mill, which has more than state-wide reputation, is in operation here. It employs

CHURCH AND SCHOOL, FAYETTEVILLE, N. C.

almost exclusively colored labor. The owners of the mill have erected for their laborers a church and a two-story schoolhouse. Through the negotiation of the writer this school has been placed at the disposition of the colored Lutheran mission free of charge. Missionary March, who had visited Fayetteville in the summer of 1913 and reported favorably to the Mission Board, moved from Southern Pines to Fayetteville in December, 1913, and opened a promising school. He also conducts the Sunday-school and divine services in the same building.

Wilmington.

Wilmington, 83 miles southeast of Fayetteville, is a seaport with a population of 29,000, one half of which is colored. Rev. Aug. Burgdorf was stationed here for a time in 1897, but on account of sickness he was compelled to resign. The field was visited in December, 1913, by Rev. March and the writer. Material for mission work is plentiful, and Rev. March has rented a corner store where he preaches twice a month. A Lutheran school will in course of time be established.

SOUTH CAROLINA.

St. Luke's, Spartanburg.

Missionary McDavid having repeatedly advised that mission work be taken up in South Carolina, with its colored population of 835,843, the writer, pursuant to instructions from the Mission

ST. LUKE'S SCHOOL, SPARTANBURG, S. C.

Board, the middle of November, 1913, also made an exploration trip into that state. Finding what he considered a promising field in Spartanburg, he advised the Board to take steps to occupy it. Rev. McDavid, of Charlotte, was requested to make the necessary arrangement. In an old shack, as nothing better could be rented, he opened a Lutheran school. Twice a month he conducts services, and Miss Wilmar Barnhardt, of Concord, N. C., took charge of the school in January, 1914.

THE EDUCATIONAL INSTITUTIONS.

From the earliest days of our Mission it was the purpose of the Board and of the missionaries to educate colored young men for our missionary work; but in the pioneer days material for the ministerial office was scarce, and the means with which to support indigent students were inadequate; yet two boys from New Orleans (1891—1892) and several from North Carolina and Virginia were sent to Springfield, Ill., to study for the ministry. Of these, five graduated and entered the office as missionaries among their people. One died a few months before graduation, and two have resigned on account of sickness. The missionaries of North Carolina and Virginia, however, were fully convinced that the colored laborers should be educated in the South, on the mission field. At the first conference of the missionaries, held in Concord, N. C., February

IMMANUEL CONFERENCE. 1900.

2—5, 1900, it was resolved to urgently petition the Mission Board to establish an educational institution in North Carolina and to present this petition to the next convention of the Synodical Conference. This matter was submitted to the convention at Cincinnati in 1898, but no action was taken. Two years later, at the meeting of Synodical Conference in Bay City, Mich., it was resolved, as the subject was rather new, to furnish the pastors and congregations of the Synodical Conference with the necessary information relative to such an institution through articles in the *Missionstaube,* which was done. In Milwaukee, 1902, the Synodical Conference resolved to establish one or two preparatory schools for the education of colored ministers and teachers. At the convention in Winona, Minn., 1904, it was resolved to appropriate

$10,000 to $15,000 for Immanuel College, N. C. It was further resolved to educate colored students entirely, in course of time, at our colored institutions and from now on to give those who desire to become teachers a complete teachers' course, and that gifted Christian girls, too, should be admitted to our institutions.

Immanuel Lutheran College, Greensboro, N. C.

At the beginning of the year 1903, the Mission Board requested the writer to establish the first colored Lutheran college in North Carolina. A class-room in the schoolhouse of Grace

FACULTY OF IMMANUEL COLLEGE, 1911.

Church at Concord was, with the permission of the congregation, transformed into a dormitory, recitation, and study, and an old dilapidated house in the rear of the church into a kitchen and dining-room. On March 2, 1903, the instruction began with 11 boys, and the full school-year on September 14. Rev. J. Ph.

IMMANUEL COLLEGE, GREENSBORO, N. C.

Schmidt, pastor of the church, and Teacher H. L. Persson rendered valuable services in the training of the boys, each giving several periods a week in the college. In 1904, the Mission Board called the St. Louis graduate F. Wahlers to Immanuel College. He was ordained and inducted into his office at Grace Church, Concord, September 11. Outside the city limits of Greensboro a real estate agent donated four acres of land to the institution, and the Board bought ten acres of him. Steps were taken to erect a suitable building for the college, for which the Synodical Conference had appropriated the money. In the expectation that the new building

FACULTY OF IMMANUEL COLLEGE, 1914.

would be completed during the next school-year, the college was reopened in Greensboro in September, 1905. For two years the college occupied two houses belonging to a colored man near the college land. Rev. John C. Schmidt, missionary in Greensboro, was entrusted by the Board with the supervision of the construction of the new building. The corner-stone was laid September 17, 1905. October 3, the same year, Rev. Prof. M. Lochner, a graduate of Concordia Seminary, St. Louis, who had been ordained in Milwaukee on September 24, was installed. A year later the Board called the St. Louis graduate H. W. Gross to the fourth professorship at Immanuel College. He was ordained in Grace Church, Greensboro, on the 14th Sunday after Trinity.

The new college building was set apart for the service of God

6

June 2, 1907. At the same time the pipe organ, built by Kilgen and Son, was dedicated at a concert given by the organist, Prof. Lochner. During the school-year 1907—1908, the theological student W. Baumhoefener, from the Seminary in St. Louis, was assistant instructor. At the convention in Chicago, 1906, the Synodical Conference resolved to give those students who desired to prepare themselves for the ministry a complete practical theological course at Immanuel College, and Rev. J. Ph. Schmidt was called to the chair of professor of Theology in addition to the writer. He was inducted into his office January 10, 1909. In the autumn of the same year Prof. Gross accepted a call to Alexandria, Va. During the school-year 1910—1911, Student W. Rohe, of Concordia Seminary, was assistant instructor. As the writer at the end of the school-year 1911, was elected to the position of Field Secretary, a new office created by the Synodical Conference at Seward, Nebr., 1910, Rev. F. Berg, of Beardstown, Ill., was called by the Board to the presidency of the College. He was inducted into his office September 6, the same year, and his son, Mr. Albert Berg, was appointed assistant instructor, a position which he still holds. In October, 1912, Rev. Prof. Lochner, after seven years of service as professor and missionary, accepted the call to a professorship in the Teachers' Seminary at Addison (now at River Forest), Ill.

Immanuel School, Greensboro, N. C.

In connection with Immanuel College a school was opened in the fall of 1906 for the neglected children of that community.

IMMANUEL SCHOOL, GREENSBORO, N. C.

A room in the Girls' Cottage was primitively furnished, and the Seniors of the college alternately volunteered as teachers. In the new college building commodious class-rooms with modern equipments were assigned to what was called the Primary Department of Immanuel College. Mr. Frank Alston, the first graduate of the Teachers' Course was placed in charge of the advanced classes, while the Senior students continued the instruction in the primary classes until Teacher E. W. Reid was reinstated. After Mr. Alston's removal to Charlotte Teacher M. N. Carter in March, 1910, was transferred from Concord to Immanuel School. Through the generosity and love of the children of the Synodical Conference a one-story brick-veneered schoolhouse, containing three large class-rooms was

TEACHER E. W. REID.

TEACHER M. N. CARTER.

erected on the college campus and dedicated November 5, 1911. The teachers of the school at present are M. N. Carter and E. W. Reid. The Misses Beulah Sutton and Mary Brown, Immanuel College graduates, each taught the school for a term.

Luther College, New Orleans, La.

Rev. F. J. Lankenau was appointed by the Mission Board to the presidency of Luther College, New Orleans. The beginning of this institution was as small and difficult as the beginning of Immanuel College in North Carolina. Professors and students had many difficulties to contend with. In the autumn of 1903, Luther College began its work in the vestry room of St. Paul's Church, a room 10×30 feet. As most of the students came from the city, there was no need of providing a dormitory. Missionaries Kretzschmar and Kossmann assisted the Rev. Lankenau in the instruction of the students. Rev. F. W. Wenzel was also for a time a coworker. In the following year the Mission Board appointed a theological student from the seminary in St. Louis assistant instructor, and Teacher R. A. Wilde gave some periods daily to the college classes. A plot of ground in the rear of the church property was purchased by the Board, and a plain, but

LUTHER COLLEGE. NEW ORLEANS, LA.

commodious frame building costing $5,000 was erected. It was dedicated November 6, 1904.

The first student to graduate from Luther College, who had taken a full Teachers' Course at our institutions, Addison, and Luther College, was Napoleon Seeberry. He graduated in June, 1904. In 1906, the faculty was strengthened by two additional professors. The Rev. F. Wenger, a St. Louis graduate

PROF. F. WENGER.   PROF. R. A. WILDE.   PROF. H. MEIBOHM.

and for six years pastor at Fair Haven, Minn., and Teacher R. A. Wilde, since 1902 engaged in St. Paul's School, were installed by Rev. Lankenau on October 7. Student J. T. Miller was appointed assistant instructor, and in 1907 was elected professor. A year later, however, he accepted a call to Concordia College, New Orleans. On the 12th Sunday after Trinity, 1908, Rev. Lankenau resigned as pastor of St. Paul's Church and President of Luther College. His successor in the college was Prof. Wenger. At the convention of the Synodical Conference in Seward, Nebr., 1910, it was resolved that Luther College henceforth serve as a preparatory school for the seminary in Greensboro. In 1910, Prof. Wenger severed his connection with the institution by accepting the pastorate of the Lutheran congregation at Frohna, Mo., and Prof. R. A. Wilde was elected President in his place. During the school-year 1910—1911 Rev. Ed. H. Schmidt assisted Prof. Wilde. Then the Board called Rev. Hugo Meibohm of Crowley, La., to Luther College. He was inducted into office October 1, 1911.

THE HIGHER EDUCATION OF COLORED GIRLS.

According to the resolution of Synodical Conference at Winona, Minn., 1904, gifted Christian girls were to be admitted to our higher educational institutions. With the exception of the first term at Concord our colleges have been coeducational. In regard to mental gifts, diligence, and deportment the female students are not inferior to the males. In New Orleans a separate building is not necessary, as the girls live at home with their parents. In North Carolina it was different. Provision had to be made for lodgings of girls that came to the college from other cities. In Concord they had board and rooms witth families, generally all with one family, and were under the supervision of the President. In Greensboro a cottage consisting of six small rooms near the college was rented as a dormitory for the girls, and the dining-hall of the college was used by both sexes. As the institution employed no servants except a cook, some girls worked in the kitchen and dining-room for their board. In the summer of 1913, the girls' dormitory at Greensboro was temporarily closed, and female students are admitted only as "Day Students." While many girls attend our colleges only for a year or two and others take the four years' Preparatory Course, there have been 6 graduates from the Teachers' Course of Luther College

WILMAR BARNHARDT.   ELIZAH JOHNSTON.   PEARL WINDSOR.

ELEANORE KING.   SOPHIE RAYMOND.   SYLVINA RAYMOND.

SOME OF THE FEMALE TEACHERS OF OUR COLORED MISSION.

and 8 from that of Immanuel. These girls have rendered the Mission valuable services as teachers. At present 8 are engaged in missionary school work. Three, one of them a principal, have positions in the public school.

CONFERENCES OF THE MISSIONARIES.

Immanuel Conference.

The first conference was called by the writer to meet at Concord, N. C., in November, 1891, and was composed of survivors of the defunct "Alpha Synod." Only one member besides the writer was able to read and write; and as two of them, a year later, retired from the ministry, this conference was discontinued. February 2—5, 1900, the missionaries of North Carolina and Virginia met at Concord and organized Immanuel Conference. According to a resolution the congregations were to be invited to send delegates to this conference, and they have generally availed themselves of the privilege. During the first years the missionaries met semiannually. Later one general conference, to which lay-delegates were admitted, and one pastors' and teachers' conference was held annually, the latter, as a rule, between Christmas and New Year or after Easter. At the general conference two days are devoted to public doctrinal discussions, which are largely attended.

MEMBERS OF LUTHER CONFERENCE, NEW ORLEANS.

Luther Conference.

The missionaries of Louisiana organized themselves into a Luther Conference at Easter, 1903. For some years no sessions were held. But since 1910 they have met regularly towards the end of October in the churches of New Orleans. The night sessions, to which all the congregations are invited, are set apart for doctrinal discussions and are very well attended. These conferences are of great blessing to both the missionaries and the congregations.

MRS. WILHELMINA HOSBOND.

Member of Mount Zion Church, New Orleans.

Mrs. Hosbond has been a member of Mount Zion Church, New Orleans, for thirty years and, with the exception of

WILHELMINA HOSBOND.

Mrs. Mary C. Wright, who was confirmed in "Sailors' Home," is the oldest member of the congregation. During these many years she has been a diligent hearer and doer of God's Word and a generous giver towards Church and charitable purposes. Her home has been an asylum for orphaned children of her rela-

tives, whom she has fed and clothed, and whom she has had
educated in Mount Zion School. She was born and brought up
in slavery times and, like the majority of the old slaves, is illiterate. Still she has acquired a good Christian knowledge and
has committed to memory many of our Lutheran hymns. Though
very old, feeble, and almost deaf, she is still a diligent attendant
at divine service.

THREE PROMINENT MEMBERS OF ST. PAUL'S CHURCH.

Louis Thomas.

Louis Thomas was one of the seven children with whom
Missionary Charles Berg opened school on Claiborne St., New Orleans, in January, 1882. He belonged to the first catechumen class
of which two besides him were confirmed, and who were the founders

LOUIS THOMAS.   EMMANUEL BURTHLONG.   PETER ROBINSON.

of St. Paul's Church. His marriage to Octavie was the first to
be solemnized publicly in the new St. Paul's Church. He has
been an active member, and from time to time an officer of the
congregation since its organization. Under God it was chiefly
through his instrumentality that the entire large Thomas family
was brought into the Lutheran Church.

Emmanuel Burthlong.

Emmanuel was one of the first pupils of St. Paul's School,
an exceptionally bright, diligent, and pious boy. After his confirmation he took a course for advanced scholars under Mr. Berg
and German from the missionary. At the age of seventeen he
was appointed teacher of the primary classes of Mount Zion School.
In the autumn of 1891 he entered Concordia Seminary, Springfield, to study for the ministry. His record as a student was
unspotted. For one year he assisted the missionaries in North

Carolina. He was a fluent speaker in both English and German, and was loved by all who knew him. A few months before his graduation, 1897, he died.

Peter Robinson.

Peter Robinson was a contemporary of Burthlong, though some years younger than he. From his manhood up he has been active as a member of St. Paul's, a zealous coworker of the missionaries, and an officer of the congregation. Since January, 1914, he is teaching the Trinity Chapel school on Elmira St. — These three young men, all Creoles, have contributed much towards the upbuilding of St. Paul's Church and School. Their parents, sisters, and brothers are members of the Lutheran Church.

THREE "OLD-TIMERS" OF BETHLEHEM, NEW ORLEANS.

Robert Dixon and *Oliver Hager* with their wives joined Bethlehem Chapel in Rev. Burgdorf's time. They are some of the oldest and most substantial members of the congregation and are

ROBERT DIXON.   OLIVER HAGER.   OLIVIA WILSON.

well known in Lutheran circles of New Orleans and in the community where they have lived for more than twenty-five years. Brother Dixon presides over the deliberations of the congregation with dignity, though not always according to parliamentary rules. At joint meetings of the churches or at public sessions of Luther Conference he takes an active part in the discussions.

Brother Hager has been janitor of the congregation as long as the writer can remember, and, like Mr. Dixon, has served the church as an officer for many years.

Mrs. Olivia Wilson is by profession a midwife and a nurse and has occasion to practice her profession also in the homes of the missionaries. She is a "mammy" of the old school.

These three "old-timers" have been the faithful coworkers of the missionaries in the upbuilding of Bethlehem.

SCOTT NORMAND, MANSURA, LA.

SCOTT NORMAND'S HOUSE.

Under the hospitable roof of Scott Normand at Mansura, La., our missionaries have frequently been entertained. Rev. F. J. Lankenau preached his first sermon at his home. Rev. W. Pretzsch, the first resident missionary at Mansura, lodged with him until the parsonage was built. He, like the majority of the congregation, is a Creole. Despite his seventy-six years, he is still active. He and his good wife nursed the writer while he was sick at their home in November, 1912.

SCOTT NORMAND.

MISCELLANEOUS.

Our Colored Mission covers a period of thirty-six years. During these years 129 missionaries and teachers, exclusive of theological students, have been engaged in the work. Most of these served only a few years, some only a few months. Two missionaries and three teachers have died in the service of the Mission. The frequent changes of laborers have retarded the progress of the work. Other hindrances have been — insufficient means, the old, dilapidated, and unsanitary buildings in which the work had to be begun and continued for years, and the nomadic tendencies of the colored people. But in spite of all these hindrances our Mission has been signally blessed by the Lord.

At present 46 congregations and preaching places are being served by 49 laborers, 23 of whom are colored ministers and teachers and 8 colored female teachers, the latter having all been educated at our own institutions. The work is being carried on in ten states: Arkansas, Georgia, Illinois, Louisiana, Mississippi, Missouri, New York, North Carolina, South Carolina, Virginia. In five of these ten states the work was taken up during the last decade. During the past five years 23 congregations and preaching places have been established, making an average of nearly 5 new places a year. At the close of the year 1913 the Mission numbered 2,434 baptized members and 1,061 communicant members. The outlook is bright. There are still upwards of 6 million churchless colored people in the land. "The harvest, truly, is plenteous, but the laborers are few; pray ye, therefore, the Lord of the harvest that He will send forth laborers into His harvest."

From 1877 to 1912 the Synodical Conference contributed $448,071.58 for Colored Mission, and our colored churches $29,606.06, this being about one half of the money which these churches have raised. The mission property, unencumbered, is valued at $115,000. The annual expenses now amount to $30,000.

AN OLD-TIME NEGRO CABIN.   AN OLD "MAMMY."
PRESENT-DAY DWELLING.

DINNER HOUR IN DIXIE LAND.

STATISTICS OF THE COLORED MISSIONS, 1877—1912.

YEAR.	RECEIPTS :		SURPLUS :	
	Synodical Conference.	Negro Congr., Schools, Colleges.	Missions-taube.	Lutheran Pioneer.
1877—1878	$ 1392.20	——	——	——
1879—1882	16240.19	——	——	——
1882—1884	7030.73	$ 32.25	$1138.03	$465.79
1884—1886	9790.03	59.00	1168.99	355.94
1886—1888	16691.78	209.15	1094.80	276.52
1888—1890	16099.38	450.20	1473.16	411.88
1890—1892	25591.60	349.35	1232.18	276.56
1892—1894	22761.84	581.09	1979.65	322.32
1894—1896	28625.65	1565.59	2018.26	181.74
1896—1898	21245.64	1052.68	2378.83	377.43
1898—1900	30993.87	2164.57	2750.91	425.50
1900—1902	27250.50	2132.91	3807.86	437.92
1902—1904	31125.50	2518.53	4410.89	450.44
1904—1906	44551.73	3788.20	4202.93	286.86
1906—1908	47437.90	4730.99	5100.72	578.74
1908—1910	45048.07	4709.75	5206.85	227.11
1910—1912	56194.97	5261.80	4478.85	148.73
	$448071.58	$29606.06	$42442.91	$ 5233.48
				42442.91

Total Surplus of both Mission Papers ....$ 47676.39

448071.58

29606.06

Grand Total Receipts for Colored Missions, 1877—1912....$525354.03

www.ingramcontent.com/pod-product-compliance
Lightning Source LLC
LaVergne TN
LVHW011214080426
835508LV00007B/775